French Literature

A Beginner's Guide

ONEWORLD BEGINNER'S GUIDES combine an original, inventive, and engaging approach with expert analysis on subjects ranging from art and history to religion and politics, and everything in between. Innovative and affordable, books in the series are perfect for anyone curious about the way the world works and the big ideas of our time.

French Literature
A Beginner's Guide

Carol Clark

ONEWORLD

A Oneworld Paperback Original

Published by Oneworld Publications 2012

ISBN 978-1-85168-899-9 (pbk)
ISBN 978-1-78074-092-8 (ebk)

Typeset by Cenveo Publisher Services, Bangalore, India
Cover design by vaguelymemorable.com
Printed and bound in Great Britain by
TJ International Ltd, Padstow, Cornwall

Oneworld Publications
185 Banbury Road
Oxford OX2 7AR
UK

Learn more about Oneworld. Join our mailing list to
find out about our latest titles and special offers at:
www.oneworld-publications.com

Contents

List of illustrations

Acknowledgements

I should like to thank my former colleagues at the University of Glasgow, Balliol College, Oxford, and the University of Oxford, first for appointing me to my Fellowship and Lectureships and then for their patience with me over many years. Their decisions allowed me to spend the best part of my working life reading great French books and discussing them with intelligent young people: a wonderful way to earn one's living.

I am also grateful to my students for their ideas and stimulation, and to the librarians at the University of Glasgow Library, the Taylor Institution Library, Oxford, the Bibliothèque Nationale (now Bibliothèque de France), Paris, and the Bibliothèque Historique de la Ville de Paris, for all their help.

I wish also to thank the Bibliothèque de France for permission to reproduce Figures 1 and 2, and Éditions Gallimard for the extract from Jean-Paul Sartre's *Le Mur* (Text 18).

Carol Clark
Oxford and Paris

Introduction

Why would one want to read French literature?

The literature of the French language is the longest-lived and richest of all European literatures apart from English. Until very recent years, it was a model for writers worldwide. Medieval French writers gave us the stories of Arthur, the Round Table and the Holy Grail, and, some would say, the ideal of romantic love. Montaigne's *Essays* have been read continuously by English speakers since they were first translated in 1603, and are still finding enthusiastic readers today. Molière's character comedy has been an inspiration for writers in England and everywhere in Europe. The realistic novel of the French nineteenth century became the model for novelists worldwide, including America and Japan, and for the structure of the feature film. The cinema itself was a French invention, and is regarded by many French people as the chief art form of the twentieth century ('le septième art'). Every century has produced its crop of poetry and prose, history, fiction, comedy and tragedy, with new forms constantly appearing as audiences changed and grew.

The readership for literature in French has never been restricted to metropolitan France. A whole French-speaking literature developed in England in the two centuries following the Norman Conquest, while in the eighteenth and early nineteenth centuries French became the language of cultivated Europe as far as Russia. The determined imposition of French language and literary study in the education systems of its former colonies produced writers who could express the feelings and experiences of distant peoples in impeccable metropolitan French, and who found readers both in their newly independent countries and in France itself – what are now called the 'post-colonial' writers. France also exports its culture around the world through the Lycée Français system.

For some readers, the word 'literature' may have taken on a somewhat forbidding sound from its appearance in syllabuses and exam specifications. Sadly, many people now think of literature as the kind of thing one has to read for an exam, rather than something one might read or listen to from choice. 'Literary' texts, they think, live in hardback books with introductions and footnotes. Though nowadays they often do, it is important to realise that none of them began their lives in this way, and not a single one of them was written to be examined on. I like to imagine Rabelais chuckling incredulously in his grave at the thought of university students answering exam questions on his stories.

I shall be trying in this book to give a sense of how the texts of the various periods took shape, what sorts of audiences they were aimed at and how they were received. I shall, obviously, have to pick out a relatively small number of authors, and shall try to show why they were the most admired in their day or afterwards, and what we can gain from reading them today. Almost every sentence here will be a generalization which specialists in the author or period discussed would want to question or qualify. This is inevitable, given the number of subjects to be covered in such a short space. Each chapter will have a small number of illustrative extracts, with accompanying English translation. The translations are my own, and are sometimes quite free – deliberately so. I shall also try, particularly in some of the illustrative texts, to show some of the ways in which readers 'used' literature in their own lives and in their relations with other people.

But what I really hope to do is help readers with little experience of French literature to find some books that they will want to read, whether in translation or (I hope) in French. One motive for doing so might be the hope of understanding France and French people better. But reading these remarkable books is a lasting pleasure in itself, and for some people the way into a lifetime of enjoyment.

1

The Middle Ages: literature before literacy

The word 'literature' comes from Latin 'litterae', letters, and to us nowadays literature always means something written down, and usually printed and published. But in the earliest days of French fiction this was not necessarily so.

French is one of the Romance languages: the languages into which spoken Latin broke up after the end of the Roman Empire. The first documents written in something recognizable as a kind of French date from AD842 and religious compositions (saints' lives, hymns) were being produced in this Old French by the end of the ninth century. By the eleventh century minstrels were performing an extensive repertoire of stirring stories to listeners, very few of whom would have been able to read.

In early medieval times long stories were almost always cast in verse, no doubt because verse is much easier to memorize than prose, and these stories were performed, without notes, to live audiences. We do not know how many of the performers themselves could read, but they certainly did not read aloud from a script.

The earliest types of story-poems are called *chansons de geste* (songs of great deeds). They purport to be true, and some do involve historical characters from much earlier periods such as Charlemagne, King of the Franks and, from the year 800, Emperor of the West. The adventures attributed to these figures are no doubt mostly invented. Each performer, though, would be retelling a story handed down by respected predecessors and might therefore believe that it was in some sense true. It is thought that these stories were sung during or after meals in lords' halls, to largely illiterate audiences of fighting men. Some singers were retainers of the lords, others were itinerant minstrels called *jongleurs.* These might compose their own poems or perform others written by poets called *trouvères,* which they learned either from hearing them recited or from written texts. Obviously some of these poet–performers must have been literate, as those poems that survive do so in written form.

The most famous *chanson de geste* is the *Chanson de Roland,* about Charlemagne's wars in Spain. Some version of this was performed before Duke William at the battle of Hastings by a *jongleur* called Taillefer. The earliest version of it that survives (in a manuscript in Oxford's Bodleian Library) is thought to have been composed in England, for a Norman audience, in the early twelfth century. The last line of the written poem says that it had been composed or performed, or perhaps simply copied, by someone called Turoldus, but we do not know anything else about him. Some 80 to 100 *chansons de geste* survive.

TEXT 1 CAVALRY TO THE RESCUE

These lines from the *Chanson de Roland* follow the battle of Roncesvalles in which the French rearguard is slaughtered, and precede the final fight in which Roland dies. The two heroes had been previously contrasted when the wise Oliver begged the brave but rash Roland to sound his horn and call Charlemagne to return with the main body of the army (lines 1051 onwards). Roland refuses to do so until the battle is almost lost (line 1702). Charlemagne hears the horn at line 1757 and the army turns back, but too late.

The poem is composed in assonanced *laisses*, which are stanzas of indeterminate length, with the last syllable of each line containing the same vowel (here /a/ and /i/).

CXXXIX

Par grant irur chevalchet li reis Charles
Desur sa brunie li gist sa blanche barbe.
Puignent ad ait tuit li barun de France
N'i ad icel ne demeint irance
Que il ne sunt a Rollant le cataigne
Ki se combat as Sarrazins d'Espaigne;
Si est blecet, ne quit que anme i remaigne.
Deus! Quels seisante humes i ad en sa cumpaigne!
Unches meillurs n'en out reis ni cataigne.

CXL

Rollant reguardet es munz e es lariz;
De cels de France I veit tanz morz gesir!
E il les pluret cum chevaler gentill:
'Seignors barons, de vos ait Deus mercit!
Tutes vos anmes otreit il pareïs!
En seintes flurs il les facet gesir!
Meillors vassals de vos unkes ne vi.
Si lungement tuz tens m'avez servit,
A oes Carlon si granz pais cunquis!
Tere de France, mult estes dulz païs,
Oï desertet a tant rubostl exill.
Barons Franceis, pur mei vos vei murir:
Jo ne vos poi tenser ne guarentir.
Aït vos Deus, ki unke ne mentit!
Oliver, frere, vos ne dei jo faillir.
De doel murrai, se altre ne m'i occit.
Sire cumpainz, alum i referir.'

[King Charles rides furiously, his white beard flowing over his burnished breastplate. All the barons of France spur their hardest; not one but is bitterly angry that they are not with Roland, the brave captain, as he fights against the Saracens of Spain. He is wounded, the soul is barely left in his body. Lord, what men are the sixty left in his company! No king or captain ever had better.

Roland looks at the mountains and the hills. Of the men of France he sees so many lying dead! And he weeps for them, like a noble knight: 'Lord barons, God have mercy upon you! To all your souls may he grant Paradise. May he make them rest among the holy flowers! Better vassals than you I never saw. You have served me so long, winning such great lands for Charles! Land of France, you are indeed a fair country, now laid waste by such a calamity. Barons of France, I have seen you die for me: I was not able to protect you or save you. God keep you, He who never lied! Oliver, my brother, I must not fail you. I shall die of grief, if I am not otherwise killed. My noble companion, let us return to the fight!']

Even more numerous are the slightly later *romans*. *Roman* is the modern French word for novel, but these stories are not in the least like modern novels. The word originally meant simply a composition in the vernacular – the contemporary spoken language – rather than Latin. *Romans* are composed in rhymed verse, usually of eight syllables, and unfold long tales of adventure in which love often plays an important part. They are thought to have been performed in settings where women had a more important role than in the predominantly male, warlike gatherings where the often bloodthirsty *chansons de geste* were sung. The *romans* fall into several families (*romans d'aventure, romans d'antiquité* and so on), but the best known and most influential on later literature are the *romans Bretons*, the ones dealing with the *matière de Bretagne*, the stories of Arthur and the knights of the Round Table. ('Bretagne' here covers the Celtic lands of Brittany and Cornwall. 'Bretagne la grant' is the island kingdom: that is the origin of the expression 'Great Britain'.)

The best poems in this group were written between 1150 and 1250. The most notable writer of them was **Chrétien de Troyes**, who is believed to have died around 1190. But the stories survived and went on being told in many different forms for hundreds of years. These tales were a key means of transmission for the social values of chivalry and courtesy (*courtoisie*: originally, the behaviour befitting members of a court, as opposed to *vilenie*, the behaviour of villeins or serfs). Another of Chrétien's stories, the *Perceval*, introduces the motif of the Grail, the quest for which will soon become the subject of many further poems. Prose versions of the tales of chivalry and of the Grail romances (for reading from a written text, we must suppose) were produced as early as the thirteenth century, but really came into their own in the late fifteenth with the invention of printing.

Medieval prose literature does exist, but apart from the works of the historians (**Froissart, Commines**) it is little read nowadays. Much of it is of religious origin: sermons, saints' lives – these exist in verse too – and books of devotion. Comic writing appears first in verse form with the *fabliaux* (late twelfth to early fourteenth century), but by the fifteenth century realistic prose writers are found engaging in mockery of everyday relationships, in works like the *Quinze joyes de mariage*.

There was no organized commercial theatre at this period: all productions were amateur, however large-scale and elaborate. Plays might be religious (*mystères, moralités*), satirical (*soties*) or broadly comical (*farces*). They were staged by student societies or confraternities of laymen. Scripts for them survive from the fourteenth century onwards.

So in medieval literature we find a variety of conflicting value systems: piety and satire, blood-lust and courtliness. In particular, the values of *amour courtois* (courtly love, placing women on a pedestal) seem completely at odds with what would later be called the *gaulois* (Gaulish – i.e. primitive) comic spirit of the *fabliaux* and farces, based on cuckoldry, randy wives, hen-pecked husbands and so forth. But it seems that these different types of composition can have been enjoyed by the same people at different times, and the clash is one that will persist in French culture for many centuries to come.

Probably the best-known French medieval poet is **François Villon** (1431–after 1463). An educated man (he took his MA in 1452 and at one point was teaching in one of the colleges of the University of Paris), he was also a thief, brawler and eventually murderer who was more than once condemned to death but always managed to escape execution. The first thirty years of his life are quite well documented in academic and legal sources, but he vanishes from the record after 1463. His chief writings are the *Petit testament* and the much longer *Grand testament*, satirical poems cast in the form of mock wills. In them he leaves his (by then non-existent) property to named figures of the time, usually in a sardonic or comically inappropriate way. The *Grand testament* is interspersed with short lyrical poems, and these are his best-known writings: among them is the *Ballade des dames du temps jadis* (Ballad of the Ladies of Former Days), with its refrain 'Mais ou sont les neiges d'antan?' (Where are the snows of yesteryear?). The language in which Villon writes is called Middle French, and should be easier to read than Old French. But in fact the main texts of the *Testaments* are very difficult as they are full of allusions and personal jokes, many obscene, aimed at the legatees. Some passages are even written in fifteenth-century thieves' slang. Modern editors have tried to tease out his meanings, but they often disagree. Villon's poems were printed soon after his disappearance by one Antoine Verard, but they were little read then. He became better known in the sixteenth century, when the satirical poet Clement Marot re-published him. The figure of

2

The sixteenth century: from Rabelais to Montaigne

It was in the sixteenth century that French literature began to take forms more familiar to us today, with the appearance of printed prose fiction, printed collections of poetry and a literature of reflection to which Michel de Montaigne first gave the name of essays.

Printing had come to France in the 1470s, soon after its invention in Germany. The main centres of the new business were Paris, particularly the university district where print shops soon supplanted the traditional trade of manuscript copying, and Lyon. At first the majority of books printed were in Latin, the language of scholarship and the Church, but certain houses soon developed a trade in vernacular works as well. Their biggest output was of works of devotion – books of hours, saints' lives, guides to a good death and the like – but more practical works like almanacs, guides to planting and home medical hints also seem to have sold well. An entertainment literature also began to develop in the form of jest-books, collections of comic or tragic tales and reworked prose versions of the tales of chivalry. The new techniques for rapid reproduction of books soon outran the available copy, and material to print and sell was dug up from all possible sources. It is not at all unusual to see a work decades or even centuries old described on a sixteenth-century title-page as 'nouvellement composé'. As well as weighty and handsome versions of the old romances, meant for the well-to-do lay market, little works of pamphlet size ('chapbooks') were also printed to be sold by itinerant pedlars (chapmen). The stories found in these books are usually far-fetched adventures, told in comically exaggerated style. One such group of tales concerned a family of giants, created by Merlin the Enchanter to serve King Arthur in battle: a kind of downmarket spin-off from the chivalric world of the *matière de Bretagne*. It is from this unlikely context that the first great work of French prose fiction, the *Pantagruel* and *Gargantua* of Rabelais, was to emerge.

Rabelais

We know little of the early life of **François Rabelais** (?1494–1552): even his date of birth has been placed as early as 1483 and as late as 1494. By 1520 he was already a professed Franciscan monk, but we do not know at what age he joined the order: possibly even as a boy. What is certain is that whatever early education he received would have been in a clerical context, and in Latin. By the time we first hear of him, he is trying to learn Greek, and petitioning the pope to be allowed to transfer to the Benedictines, who were more sympathetic to humanist as well as to purely theological studies. The move to the Benedictines did not, it seems, cure François' restlessness, since by 1530 he was on leave of absence from his monastery, studying medicine at the Faculty in Montpellier. The subject at this time was, of course, largely studied out of classical texts (Rabelais himself was to lecture on Hippocrates and Galen), but more practical approaches were coming to be considered: dissection was beginning to be used, and Rabelais is credited with designing a device for setting and straightening broken legs. In 1532 he was appointed chief doctor at the Hôtel-Dieu, the main hospital at Lyon.

It was while at the Hôtel-Dieu that he published his first fictional work, the *Horribles et espouventables faicts et prouesses du tresrenomme Pantagruel* of 1532. It is an odd little book, sixty-four 11x15cm leaves (128 pages) of blackletter (about 40,000 words), weighing only a couple of ounces. The decoration of the title-page (Figure 1) had first been used for a serious legal textbook, but then re-used for a satirical account of the progress of the new disease, syphilis (the *Triumphe de haulte et puissante Dame Verolle*). Obviously syphilis was a topical subject for humour, and there are plenty of jokes about it in the *Pantagruel* as well. But the main structure of the story is thoroughly traditional. Like many *chansons de geste* (the ones called *Enfances* of this or that hero) it recounts the birth, infancy, childhood, education and first feats of arms of the giant prince Pantagruel, up to his entry into his kingdom. Much of the humour is based on the giant's huge size, which, however, varies greatly from one chapter to another. But there is also much topical satire, and a degree of unbridled fantasy unmatched in any fiction of the time, or probably of any other.

Who could have considered such a book worth buying? Not serious fathers of families, but perhaps young men, students or apprentices hoping for the social and sexual success that came from having a fund of stories and jokes to draw on in male or mixed company. Certainly this is how Rabelais promotes his first book in the tongue-in-cheek prologue to *Pantagruel*: he reminds his readers what faith they had placed in the *Grandes et inestimables chroniques de l'énorme géant Gargantua* (a chapbook published some months before), and how they had won the favour of ladies by telling them long, exciting stories taken from that work. Gentlemen, he says, can also cheer themselves up on unsuccessful hunting trips by telling over Gargantua's adventures. The book could be medically valuable as well, the narrator says. (We remember that medical hints were an important sub-genre of early printed literature, but Rabelais, as a university-educated doctor,

Figure 1 Rabelais, *Pantagruel*, 1532, title-page

would have had little respect for these). Wrapped in hot cloths and applied to the face, he says, the book will cure toothache! But its chief value has been to people taking the sweating cure for syphilis: stuck in their tubs, 'their only consolation was to be read to out of the said book'. Now he, the author, 'your humble slave'; is offering us another book of the same type, 'except that it is a little more truthful and credible than the other'. In fact, it is immensely more far-fetched and improbable.

Rabelais' prologue makes fun of contemporary prologues and title-pages with their recurring claims of usefulness. But it allows us to notice one thing that is not misleading: the way in which most people's experience of fiction, and in fact of poetry also, was not yet a matter of silent, private reading, but was embedded in a social context – being read to or reading to others, selecting and interpreting elements from printed fiction for one's own oral performance. The use of printed fiction in these ways did not wholly die out until well into the nineteenth century.

Pantagruel was followed by a 'prequel' *Gargantua* (1534), which brings back the hero of the original chapbook, the *Grandes et inestimables chroniques,* but takes him from the mists of Arthurian antiquity and places him in a more modern context, his youth just preceding the invention of printing. The same *enfances* structure is used as in *Pantagruel*, but the babyhood and early childhood of the hero are treated at much greater length: *Gargantua* is the first work of fiction to show any but the most perfunctory interest in this stage of life – perhaps because of the scope it gave for the scatological humour dear to Rabelais's heart. The young Gargantua's studies are also treated at unusual length, allowing for much satire of the still medieval University of Paris. Then follow the call to arms, the mighty battles of thousands of cavalry and infantry – all fought, for some reason, over some twenty square miles of the rural region of France where Rabelais grew up – and the triumphal entry into adulthood.

TEXT 2 A GIANT'S FIRST VISIT TO PARIS

Chapter XVI of *Gargantua* sees the young prince arriving to study in Paris with his tutor, page and servants, and ends with them 'refreshing' themselves with a banquet and wine. Chapter XVII purports to explain how the city got its name –'par rys' (for a joke) and 'Paris' sound the same in French – though it was already being referred to by that name by characters in the story long before Gargantua's arrival there. Such deliberate inconsistencies are characteristic of Rabelais' storytelling. Giant tales usually credit the giants with having created various landscape features and/or having given them their names (as here, in Chapter XV, the plain of Beauce).

> Comment Gargantua paya sa bienvenue es Parisiens
> et comment il print les grosses cloches de l'eglise
> Nostre Dame.
> Chapitre XVII

Quelques jours après qu'ilz se feurent refraischiz, il visita la ville et fut veu de tout le monde en grande admiration, car le people de Paris est tant sot, tant badault et tant inepte de nature, qu'un basteleur, un porteur de rogatons, un mullet avecques ses cymbales, un vielleur au milieu d'un carrefour, assemblera plus de gens que ne feroit un bon prescheur evangelicque.

Et tant molestement le poursuivirent qu'il feut contrainct soy reposer suz les tours de l'eglise Nostre Dame. Auquel lieu estant, et voyant tant de gens à l'entour de soy, dist clerement :

'Je croy que ces marroufles voulent que je leur paye ici ma bienvenue et mon *proficiat.* C'est raison. Je leur voys donner le vin, mais ce ne sera que par rys.'

Lors, en soubriant, destacha sa belle braguette, et, tirant sa mentule en l'air, les compissa si aigrement qu'il en noya deux cens soixante mille quatre cens dix et huyt, sans les femmes et petiz enfans.

Quelque nombre d'iceulx evada ce pissefort à legiereté des pieds, et quand furent au plus hault de l'Université, suans, toussans, crachans et hors d'haleine, commencerent à renier et jurer, les ungs en cholere, les aultres par rys: 'Carymary, carymara! Par saincte Mamye, nous sommes baignez par rys!' Dont fut depuis la ville nommée *Paris*.

How Gargantua celebrated his arrival with the Parisians and how he took away the great bells of the church of Notre Dame
Chapter XVII

After they had rested for a few days, he went out to see the town and was seen with great amazement by everyone, for the population of Paris is so foolish, so idly curious and so naturally stupid that a tumbling actor, a pardoner, a mule with its bells or a fiddler in the middle of a crossroads will draw a bigger crowd than a good gospel preacher could hope to do.

And they followed him about in such a tiresome fashion that he was obliged to take refuge on the towers of Notre Dame. Once he was there, looking down and seeing so many people about him, he said in a clear voice, 'I think these clowns want me to thank them for my welcome and give them something to remember me by. That's only right. Well, the drink's on me, but the joke will be on them'.

Then, with a big smile, he undid his fine codpiece and, waving his penis in the air, he pissed on them so violently that he drowned two hundred and sixty thousand four hundred and eighteen of them, not counting the women and little children.

Some of them ran fast enough to escape this mighty wave of piss, and when they reached the top of the University hill, sweating, coughing, spitting and out of breath, they began to curse and swear, some in anger and others laughing, saying, 'By the mass, the joke's on us! Fiddle-de-dee, we're drowned in pee!' And so the town was called Paree.]

After *Gargantua* Rabelais left off writing fiction for twelve years to follow a busy career in medicine and diplomacy, living in Italy for several years as personal physician and secretary to the Cardinal du Bellay. When he returned to fiction it was to take his book in very different directions. He seems still to regard it as all the same book, since the two further volumes published in his lifetime were given the titles of *Le Tiers livre* and *Le Quart livre* (of Pantagruel's *Chronicles*), and they feature the same cast of characters, but having adventures of a new kind. The *Tiers livre* marks the greatest departure from his previous style: it contains little of the humour based on size, and none of the bloodthirsty battle sequences, that drove the first two volumes. In the first volume Pantagruel, the giant prince, had acquired a normal-sized sidekick called Panurge, a disreputable perpetual-student character. Panurge vanishes from the action in *Gargantua*, since that takes place before Pantagruel's birth: the giant's sidekick in that volume is a two-fisted monk called Frère Jean des Entommeures. In the *Tiers livre*, however, in defiance of chronology, Panurge and Frère Jean are brought together as members of Pantagruel's household: like a comic-book character, Frère Jean does not seem to have got any older and they make a classic brain-and-brawn pairing, constantly arguing. Panurge is now at the centre of the story: he does seem to have aged somewhat, and now announces that it is time for him to marry and settle down. Just one question troubles him: 'Serai-je cocu?' (Will my wife cheat on me?). In the world of broad comedy that these characters inhabit, there is only one answer to that question: yes. Nevertheless, Pantagruel takes Panurge's problem seriously, and the band embarks on a series of consultations of various authorities and interpretations of their pronouncements, which occupies the rest of the volume. Wilfully blanking out the answer that is staring him in the face, Panurge remains unconvinced, so the band then takes ship for a journey around the world to try to find and consult the oracle of the *Dive Bouteille* (the Bottle Goddess). This journey occupies the *Quart livre*.

It is clear that the two later books deal in comedy of a more intellectual kind, although battle scenes and comedy of size reappear in the *Quart livre*, alongside a new kind of surreal humour based on word-play. Rabelais died shortly after the publication of the *Quart livre* in 1552; the characters' adventures were brought to some kind of conclusion in a *Cinquième livre* published in 1569 (the Bottle Goddess's oracular pronouncement is 'TRINCH' – drink – which seems to please everyone). But this volume is now considered not to be Rabelais's work, except perhaps for some short sections. It was, however, part of the 'Rabelais' that Swift, Sterne or Flaubert read and admired.

Court life and religious war

The first half of the sixteenth century had been a period of consolidation of the French monarchy and of peace within the national boundaries, though French armies had been involved in warfare in Italy. The king, François I, and the great nobles replaced their fortified castles with beautiful *châteaux* in the Renaissance style, and imported Italian painters, sculptors and goldsmiths, including Leonardo da Vinci and Benvenuto Cellini, to adorn them. The arts of music, dancing and ceremonial jousting were brought to a high point in this courtly culture, and the poetry it produced was equally stylised, with the Petrarchan, idealizing vein of love poetry preferred. The greatest poet of this period was **Pierre de Ronsard** (1524–85), who wrote several volumes of love poetry (mostly sonnets, many soon made available with musical settings for ladies and gentlemen to perform), but also political and even scientific poetry. Some historians of literature refer to this period as 'le beau seizième siècle'. But it came to an abrupt end in 1559 when Henri II, François I's son, in the course of a splendid tournament and under the eyes of his wife and his mistress, was run through the eye by an opponent's splintered lance and died shortly afterwards. His heir, the sickly François II (husband of Mary, Queen of Scots) reigned for only a year, and was succeeded by another boy king, Charles IX, aged ten, with their mother Catherine de Médicis (of the Florentine family) as regent. Charles died at twenty-four without issue, to be succeeded by yet another childless brother, Henri III. The Queen Mother was therefore a power behind the throne for thirty years, dying in the same year as the third of her sons to be king was assassinated. A succession of underage kings, leading to a concentration of power in the hands of a woman, was seen as a catastrophe for the nation, and the most powerful nobles took it as the opportunity to assert their own power against that of the throne.

In France, as in England and Germany, the 1520s and 1530s had seen movements of religious reform, and François I had been quite sympathetic to these. But when the Protestants came to acquire political power in some cities, aand certain great nobles joined the reform party, the question of whether to allow the Protestants freedom of worship became more doubtful. After the death of Henri II, political stability appeared threatened, and some of Catherine's advisers wished to suppress Protestantism by force. The queen at first seemed to favour toleration, but talks with the Protestants broke down and 1562 marked the beginning of the Wars of Religion, a series of civil conflicts that waxed and waned with few interruptions for the next thirty years. They reached a peak of horror in 1572 with the Massacre of St Bartholomew's Day, when Catholic mobs turned on the Protestants in Paris and other cities, killing many hundreds of them in a single night.

These decades of religious conflict produced a new religious and polemical literature. It was one of the tenets of the Reform that Christians should read the Bible and interpret it for themselves, and that they should pray and preachers should preach in the vernacular and not in Latin. We therefore find new translations of the Bible into French and French metrical psalms prepared for singing by poets like **Clément Marot** (1496–1544), otherwise a writer of love poetry and satires. **Jean Calvin** (1509–1564) translated his *Christianae religionis institutio* (1536) into French in 1541, using language simple and clear enough for lay people to understand. He also wrote various polemical treatises in even more familiar style (his *Traîté des reliques* is particularly knockabout). Protestant political thinkers produced angry treatises and Catholic controversialists replied, in French as well as Latin, and polemical poetry was written on both sides. The most memorable work of this kind is *Les Tragiques* by **Agrippa d'Aubigné** (1552–1630), an epic treatment in seven books of the sufferings of the Protestants. It was written in the 1580s but could not be published until 1616.

Montaigne

After Rabelais, the other sixteenth-century prose writer who is still widely read in French, and also in English and many other languages, is **Michel de Montaigne** (1534–92), whose adult life unfolded against this background of religious strife, and who was influenced by it to form a sceptical and individualistic outlook.

We know much more about Montaigne as a person than about Rabelais, partly because at one stage he played a well-documented role in public life, but mostly because a fair part of his book, the *Essais*, is self-descriptive – something very unusual for the time. He also kept a diary during a journey through Germany and Italy in 1580–82 which was discovered and published in the eighteenth century. Undertaking such a journey simply for pleasure and interest was then also a very unusual thing for a man of his rank and age to do.

Montaigne was the eldest son of a landed family near Bordeaux, where his château of Montaigne can still be visited.

His was not an ancient family, however. His great-grandfather had been a Bordeaux merchant called Eyquem; his grandfather was the first to buy land and his father the first to serve the crown as a soldier (both necessary steps on the way to noble status) and to style himself Pierre Eyquem de Montaigne. Michel was the first to drop the Eyquem. His father seems to have intended him to join the *noblesse de robe,* the intermediary caste of lawyers and civil servants, and many of Montaigne's lifelong friends did belong to this group. However Michel had other ideas for himself. Having, it is believed, studied the law and certainly served as a magistrate until the age of thirty-seven, he then withdrew to his estate. His plan, however, was not to lead the life of a country squire. He boasts his complete ignorance of, and lack of interest in, estate management. In an inscription on his library wall he describes himself as thoroughly fed up (*pertaesus*) with the law and about to dedicate himself to the service of the Muses. He is going to read: the classics, modern history, poetry. This he proceeds to do, acquiring in the course of his life some thousand volumes, an enormous number for the time. Some 300 of these survive, with his signature in them and sometimes also marginal notes.

Like Rabelais's *Chronicles*, Montaigne's is a work that took shape over a long period of time. We believe that he started writing what would eventually become the *Essais* in 1572, but with little idea of what the book would eventually turn into. It was published for the first time in 1580, at Bordeaux, as a work in two volumes, Book I of fifty-six chapters varying between short and medium length, and Book II with short and medium chapters and one disproportionately long one, Book II chapter 12, which is almost a book in its own right. In 1588 a new edition included a Book III of thirteen further chapters, all quite long, and also a great many additions to the existing chapters of Book I and Book II. Even then Montaigne did not stop rereading and rewriting his book. Working on unbound sheets of the 1588 edition, he added a great many further, hand-written observations, seemingly in preparation for a third version of the *Essais,* which however he did not live to see through the press. It was eventually published in 1595 with a preface by a young woman whom he referred to as his adopted daughter (though formal, legal adoption did not exist in France in his time), Marie de Gournay.

The resulting three books therefore reflect Montaigne's changing interests and opinions over a period of twenty years. He rarely cut anything he had written, at least after 1580, but added illustrative examples and second and third layers of obser-vation, which sometimes seem to contradict what he has just said (that is, what he had written ten or twenty years previously). The resulting text can be confusing, and most modern editions attempt to separate the various layers of composition with signs like *a, b, c* or /, //, ///. Readers between 1595 and 1907 had to deal with the text in its unseparated form, however, and do not seem to have found it too daunting.

Book I, chapter 8, *De l'oisiveté* (About Idleness) describes the early stages of his project of self-education. The result of his at first completely aimless wandering among books, he says, was to fill his head with so many incongruous ideas ('chimères et monstres fantasques') that he decided – we do not know exactly when – to write down his responses to his reading, at first simply in the order they occurred to him ('les mettre en rolle'). Some of the earliest, shortest, chapters of the *Essais* do seem to have been put together in this way. But soon he is writing longer, more struc-tured pieces, some of them on traditional debating subjects like death, pain, custom, friendship or the upbringing of children. Right from the beginning, however, his attitude to these subjects, and his style in discussing them, are unorthodox. His approaches are often sceptical, humour intrudes in unlikely places, and instead of quoting his classical authors as authorities, he engages in lively debate with them, even the ones he most admires.

With the passing of time, and particularly after the publication of the 1580 edition and its unexpected success with readers, Montaigne comes to realise that what he has produced is a kind of changing portrait of his mind and its workings, and he begins to say that this was his intention all along. Passages of self-description and self-analysis, and reflections on the process of writing, become more frequent, though they are certainly never preponderant.

At the beginning, Montaigne liked to think of himself as a private person. Why, then, was he using the new technology of print to communicate his thoughts to strangers? At first (II, 17, 1580) he says that it is simply for the benefit of his family, so that they will have a memento of him after he is dead. Printing his book is quicker and simpler than having it copied out by hand. But by the 1590s he is sounding like a modern blogger: his best friend having died, he says, there is no one to whom he can communicate his thoughts by letter, so he is launching them on the print sphere in the hope of finding like-minded readers. In III, 10, he even suggests that such a reader need only write to him and 'I will come and bring him Essays in flesh and blood'.

Something of the kind did in fact happen. Marie Le Jars de Gournay read the *Essais* in her château in Picardy and, determined to meet the author, travelled to a political conference at Blois where she knew Montaigne would be – an astonishing thing for a young unmarried woman to do at this time. They met and became lifelong friends; Marie returned to Montaigne where she lived with Montaigne's family, including his mother, serving first as an amanuensis, then a collaborator and finally, with Pierre de Brach, preparing the 1595 edition of the *Essais* and writing its preface. She continued to be a writer, moved to Paris, never married and, most unusually for a woman at the time, lived by her pen, dying in 1645.

The mention of a political conference reminds us that, so far from being a literary recluse, the Proust of the sixteenth century,

Montaigne led an active public life, including being twice elected mayor of Bordeaux and acting as a diplomatic contact between the Catholic King Henri III and his Protestant cousin and eventual successor Henry of Navarre during the Wars of Religion. These wars indeed become the subject of some of the most trenchantly written passages of the *Essais*. A moderate and traditionalist, despite or perhaps because of his sceptical cast of mind, Montaigne was horrified to see his country dissolved into bloodshed and chaos, all in the name of reform.

The *Essais* treat every subject under the sun – the old dinnertable taboos of sex (III, 5), politics (I, 23 and in many other places) and religion (I, 56; III, 2), but also the upbringing of children, both boys (I, 26) and girls (III, 5), philosophy (I, 20), history and poetry (II, 10), witchcraft (III, 11), the colonizing of the Americas (I, 20; III, 6), animal intelligence (II, 12) … In fact, it is quite artificial to assign particular subjects to particular chapters, as any subject can be discussed anywhere. In Book III especially, the titles of chapters give little clue to what they will contain: sex is treated under the heading 'On Some Verses of Virgil', and the witchcraft trials that disfigured Montaigne's century in a chapter called 'About Lame People'. Book II chapter 12, purporting to be a defence of Christian belief, is a wonderful grab-bag that includes some of Montaigne's most eloquent writing on history, politics and religion alongside anecdotes of logical foxes and lovelorn elephants.

TEXT 3 THE BOOK OF THE WORLD

Chapter 26 of Book I of Montaigne's *Essais* is addressed to a noble lady, pregnant at the time of writing, and offers her advice on the upbringing of her son-to-be – for, says Montaigne, she is 'too spirited to begin otherwise than with a boy'. (He does make some very pertinent comments on the upbringing of girls elsewhere, in chapter 5 of Book III).

Most sixteenth-century treatises on education stress the learning of Latin and Greek, and the importance of reading ancient literature and history as a preparation for one's own rhetorical performances. Though himself well-read in the classics, Montaigne argues that a noble boy does not need to have a scholar's upbringing: he will read with a tutor (Montaigne did not approve of schools) and, as soon as he is old enough, also travel with him.

Il se tire une merveilleuse clarté, pour le jugement humain, de la fréquentation du monde. Nous sommes tous contraints et amoncellez en nous, et avons la veuë racourcie à la longueur de nostre nez. On demandoit à Socrate d'où il estoit. Il ne repondit pas 'D'Athenes', mais : 'Du monde'. Luy, qui avoit son imagination plus pleine et plus estanduë, embrassoit l'univers comme sa ville, jettoit ses connoissances, sa société et ses affections à tout le genre humain : non pas comme nous qui ne regardons que sous nous.

Quand les vignes gelent en mon village, mon prebstre en argumente l'ire de Dieu sur la race humaine, et juge que la pepie en tienne des-jà les Cannibales. A voir nos guerres civiles, qui ne crie que cette machine se bouleverse et que le jour du Jugement nous prend au collet, sans s'aviser que plusieurs pires choses se sont veuës, et que les dix mille parts du monde ne laissent pas de galler le bon temps cependant? [...] A qui il gresle sur la teste, tout l'hemisphere semble estre en tempeste et orage. [...]

Mais qui se presente, comme dans un tableau, cette grande image de nostre mere nature en son entiere magesté; qui lit en son visage une si generale et constante varieté : qui se remarque là dedans, et non soy, mais tout un royaume, comme un traict d'une pointe très-delicate: celuy-là seul estime les choses selon leur juste grandeur.

Ce grand monde, que les uns multiplient encore comme especes soubs un genre, c'est le mirouër où il nous faut regarder pour nous connoistre de bon biais. Somme, je veux que ce soit le livre de mon escholier.

[Human judgment is wonderfully clarified by a knowledge of the world. We are all hemmed in and piled up in ourselves, and cannot see beyond the ends of our noses.

When they asked Socrates where he was from, he replied, not 'Athens' but 'the world'. He, with his far-ranging imagination, embraced the universe as his home city, sharing his knowledge, his society and his feelings with all of humanity, unlike us who look only at what is under our feet. When the vines freeze in my village, my parish priest preaches God's wrath against the human race, and imagines they've already got the pip in Timbuctoo. When we look at our civil wars, who does not cry out that the whole earth is turned upside down, and the day of judgment has us by the throat, without reflecting that many worse things have happened, and that ten thousand parts of the world are still enjoying life while we suffer? ... Someone with hailstones falling on his head thinks that the whole hemisphere is caught in storm and tempest ...

But the man who holds before him, as if in a picture, that great image of our mother nature in all her majesty; who reads in her face such general and constant change; who sees himself in it, and not just himself but a whole kingdom, as the mark of a tiny brush-point: he alone sees things in their just proportion.

This great world, which some believe to be but one of many such, is the mirror in which we must look to know ourselves rightly. In a word, it is the book I want my pupil to learn from].

Some aspects of sixteenth-century writing therefore look back towards the Middle Ages, while others point forward to the preoccupations of the eighteenth century, and even later times. Lively discussion of some of Montaigne's ideas is even now in progress on the internet (see p. 195).

3
The seventeenth century: dramatists and moralists

Henri de Bourbon, the Protestant King of Navarre, became heir presumptive to the throne of France on the death of the last of Henri III's brothers (Catherine de Medici's sons) in 1584. But when the king himself was assassinated in 1589, Henri had to fight for the throne against the fanatical Catholic party, the Ligue. When he agreed in 1593 to renounce Protestantism and reign as a Catholic king, his rights were recognized by most parties, though the Ligue, supported by Spain, continued to fight a rearguard action. (It was at this time that he is supposed to have said 'Paris vaut bien une messe', Paris is worth a mass.)

Once established in his kingship, Henri IV proved a wise and popular ruler, and under him France enjoyed more peace than it had known for many years, until he was assassinated in a Paris street by a Ligue supporter in 1610. In 1598 Henri had issued the Edict of Nantes, giving a degree of toleration to Protestants and designating certain cities as places of safety for them: this measure remained in force until 1685.

Henri was succeeded by his son Louis XIII who was able to hold the kingdom together, extend its frontiers, centralize and firmly establish royal power, all thanks to the political genius of Cardinal Richelieu, his first minister from 1624 to 1642, who was also an important patron of the arts and literature. When Richelieu died, he was succeeded by another cardinal, the Italian

Mazarin, favourite of the widowed queen, Anne of Austria. Louis XIII died in 1643, leaving two sons, born in 1638 and 1640. (His marriage had been childless for twenty-four years – until, some said, the dashing Italian cardinal appeared on the scene). The elder boy succeeded as Louis XIV: he was to reign until 1715, build Versailles, patronize the arts and theatre on a grand scale and personify what the French call *le grand siècle*.

But as a child he had to accept the regency of his mother and the control of Mazarin, whose unpopularity was such as to provoke two short revolts in Paris known as the first and second *Frondes*, in 1648 and 1651. At these times the queen and her son had to flee Paris and the threat of the mob. It was not surprising, then, that on the death of Mazarin in 1661 the twenty-three-year-old king announced that he would not be replaced: he, Louis, would reign personally. No royal minister was ever to be so powerful again as Richelieu and Mazarin had been. The great nobles of the traditional landed aristocracy had shown themselves unreliable in the second *Fronde* and Louis came to rely more on men of his own creation, a class of royal servants sprung from the *noblesse de robe* (the lawyer caste) and even the bourgeoisie, like his great finance minister Colbert. Louis also decided to move the centre of royal power from the Louvre in Paris (with its painful memories of the *Frondes*) to a purpose-built palace on the site of an existing hunting lodge at Versailles, about ten miles from the city. Building of the new palace, begun in 1661, was complete in 1668, but further extensions were begun almost immediately and the court was not established there permanently until 1678. Even then, building and landscaping continued until 1710, by which time the palace had taken on something very like the shape we see today. By this time, too, anyone seeking advancement (offices, great or small, in the king's service, sinecures, jobs for their relatives – these were the only openings for aristocrats who were not willing to forfeit their status by taking on productive work) had to be physically present at Versailles to hope to

put on by more or less stable groups of actors (of both sexes, unlike in England or Spain at this time), often related by blood or marriage, who signed articles of association and were collectively responsible for all the expenses of the production. They had first to rent acting space (indoor tennis-courts were often used for this purpose), then provide themselves with a text to perform, either by buying a script outright from a *poète dramatique* (the most usual method) or, if he had already a reputation, by promising him a cut of the profits. Having provided their own sets, costumes and props, and hired anyone else needed for the production – extras, doorkeepers, lighting (candle) men etc – they went into rehearsal. There was no one in the company equivalent to the modern director: the leading actors seem to have argued out between them how scenes were to be played, each expecting a certain number of 'big moments', and to be able to call on particular effects that the audience expected from them. After each performance the takings were counted, expenses deducted, and what was left divided among the company members on the basis of perhaps two shares for the leads (and one or two for the poet), one share for the junior members of the company and half a share for the most junior. Corneille's play *L'Illusion comique* actually shows a theatre troupe doing this.

The first seventeenth-century commercial dramatist whose plays survive is **Alexandre Hardy** (*c.*1570–1632), *poète à gages* (hired poet) to a troupe of actors who first toured the provinces and then settled at the Hôtel de Bourgogne, the only purpose-built theatre at that time (it had been built in the mid-sixteenth century for the purpose of staging mystery and miracle plays). Hardy is believed to have written or rewritten several hundred plays, of which thirty-four survive: tragedies, comedies, tragi-comedies, histories, pastorals, tragical-comical-historical-pastorals.... He is a kind of Shakespeare without the genius, or even great talent. But this is where modern French theatre begins.

Corneille

The eldest of France's three great dramatists of the seventeenth century was **Pierre Corneille** (1606–84). Born at Rouen of a family of magistrates and himself originally educated for the law, he began to write for the theatre in 1629, his first plays being produced by the company of the actor Mondory at the new theatre in the then (and now once more) fashionable Marais district of Paris. These early plays were comedies (romantic comedies like Shakespeare's, rather than plays chiefly meant to make the audience laugh). After his first tragedy of *Médée,* he went to Spain for the subject of *Le Cid* (1637), which was first published as a *tragi-comédie* and only subsequently as a *tragédie*. It is adapted from a Spanish play of 1621, itself based on the semi-mythical adventures of El Cid Campeador, the champion of Castile against the Moors. The plot, based on love, honour and vengeance, is the pretext for much splendid rhetoric and allows the development of the kind of moral dilemmas that became Corneille's trademark. In a middle-period Corneille tragedy everyone is noble, but these admirable characters are placed in inextricable double-binds, situations of moral conflict where they must choose between good and good: often, between a high-minded kind of love and family honour and duty. Here, for example, Rodrigue (Le Cid) loves Chimène, but is obliged by family honour to fight a duel with her father, in which he kills him. Refusing the duel for love of Chimène is not an option, since Rodrigue would then lose his honour and Chimène would stop loving him for that reason. Once her father is dead, Chimène must petition the king for Rodrigue's death, though she loves him and in fact wishes him to live. The king spares Rodrigue because of his heroic actions against the Moors, and gives Chimène a year to decide whether she will marry Rodrigue or not, so that the possibility of a 'happy' ending (tragicomedy rather than tragedy) is held open.

If one takes one's model of tragedy from ancient Greece, or even from Shakespeare, this is plainly not a tragedy at all. Not only does it not end with the deaths of the central characters, but the plot is driven chiefly by love, and whereas a Greek tragedy leaves us with a sense of human powerlessness faced with the almost arbitrary actions of the gods, here the human characters seem to be in heroic control of their actions at all times. However Corneille's idea of what constituted a tragedy was very different from ours. The plot of the play had to put *quelque grand intérêt d'Etat* (some great interest of state) in the balance, and the characters, usually princes or great generals, had to be larger than life, admirable (if only for the extremity of their wickedness) and eloquent. His plays all meet these criteria.

Le Cid was a huge success with audiences, but (perhaps for that reason) encountered much criticism from other dramatists. It was at this time that a theory of drama, and particularly of tragedy, began to be worked out in France. Cardinal Richelieu, as well as reorganizing and masterminding the government of France, had decided to create new and more elevated forms of literature and theatre, and to regularize and purify the French language. To this end he had founded the Académie Française (which still meets) for that purpose. One of the first tasks he gave them was to pronounce on the newly successful play: the *Sentiments de l'Académie française sur le Cid* appeared in 1638. It included many detailed criticisms of construction and style, but its chief objection was moral: to Chimène's unmaidenly willingness even to consider marriage to the man who had caused her father's death.

French dramatic theory as it developed from the 1640s onwards addressed both moral and formal issues. A good play (in practice, a tragedy: theorists had much less to say about comedy) should be morally improving; it should meet the (often mutually contradictory) criteria of *vraisemblance* (lifelikeness, plausibility) and *bienséance* (decorum, characters behaving in ways conventionally acceptable for their sex, age and station). In the interests of *vraisemblance*, the action should be fitted into a short space of time (ideally, the real time of performance, but in practice twenty-four hours were allowed) and take place in a single location. Plots should be simple, with no separate sub-plots. These three requirements were later summed up as the 'three unities' (of time, place and action), and were attributed to the authoritative figure of Aristotle in his *Poetics*. Stage language, along with declamation and gesture, was to be markedly different from the language of every day, just as the characters of tragedy – kings, military leaders, heroes of ancient legend – are elevated beyond everyday life. In practice, French seventeenth-century tragedies, and most comedies, are written in alexandrine couplets (twelve-syllable lines rhyming *aa, bb*, etc.), with a very restricted vocabulary. Everyday, prosaic – let alone 'low' – things are never mentioned, just as characters in tragedy never eat, sleep, touch each other or even (with very few exceptions) sit down while on stage. Any violence (fights, stabbing etc.) must take place offstage.

Corneille found many of these restrictions irksome (not, however, the prescription of alexandrine verse, of which he was a great master), and he attempts to reconcile Aristotle's supposed teaching with the demands of contemporary stage performance in his *Trois discours du poème dramatique* (1660).

The four tragedies traditionally considered Corneille's greatest (*Le Cid, Horace, Cinna* and *Polyeucte)* were all written between 1637 and 1642, in the last years of the reign of Louis XIII. The latter three all have subjects taken from Roman history, and Corneille was traditionally admired for his depiction of stern Roman virtue. He went further afield (including to Greek legend) for the subjects of his later tragedies, and their plots are often more far-fetched and convoluted, with deep-dyed villains including some memorable villainesses. He published thirty-two plays altogether.

Molière

'Molière' was the stage name of **Jean-Baptiste Poquelin** (1622–73). He was the son of a prosperous businessman, upholsterer by appointment to the king: a position that his son would have stood to inherit. But his father seems to have had even higher ambitions for him, since he was educated at the best school in Paris, the Jesuit Collège de Clermont, alongside sons of the aristocracy. Imagine, therefore, his father's feelings when Jean-Baptiste left home at twenty-one to join a troupe of actors, signing articles of association in 1643. The new company first tried to make its name in Paris but got into financial difficulties over the lease of acting space. After a short spell of imprisonment for debt, Molière left with his troupe for the provinces, where they toured for thirteen years. It is notable that although he was initially one of the younger members of the troupe he soon became their recognized leader.

Returning to Paris in 1658, they were lucky enough to be spotted and receive royal patronage. From then until 1673 Molière maintained a theatre in Paris, producing plays for a town audience composed of both aristocrats and *bourgeois*. The company was also frequently summoned to perform at one of the palaces or hunting lodges of the king or other great nobles, before an entirely aristocratic audience. These invitations could come at very short notice; the company might be asked to perform one of their town successes, but new material would also be expected. Molière's one-act play *L'Impromptu de Versailles* shows the company struggling with just such a last-minute commission.

The pinnacle of Molière's career, in terms of material and social success, was in 1664, when he was called upon to provide the acted element in the three-day festival (including cavalcades, ballets, a banquet for six hundred and fireworks) called *Les Plaisirs de l'île enchantée* (the Pleasures of the Magic Island), given before the queen and the court to show off the new gardens of the

Figure 2 Molière, *Oeuvres*, 1666, vol. I, frontispiece

then still-old Versailles, and possibly also to celebrate the king's relationship with his new mistress, Mlle de la Vallière. For this celebration Molière wrote, as well as occasional verse, a romantic comedy with singing and dancing, *La Princesse d'Elide*. After the first three days many courtiers stayed on for further entertainments, and three more of Molière's plays were put on: two already known to the audience, but one that had not been performed in public before, *Tartuffe*.

Most of Molière's plays up to this point (he had published eleven between returning to Paris in 1658 and the *Plaisirs de l'île enchantée* in 1664) had been either one- or three-act prose plays of a farcical character, or five-act romantic verse comedies in the Spanish or Italian vein. Produced quickly, they had to include a leading role for himself (he played the lead in all of his own plays, and originally in those of other writers too) and suitable parts for all the other members of the company. Audiences evidently liked to see their favourite actors developing a familiar role each time. Unsurprisingly, therefore, Molière relied on the stock plot of European comedy since classical times: young lovers separated by misunderstandings or parental oppression, but re-united with the help of sympathetic, clever servants. At the start of his Paris career Molière's role was that of the clever manservant, Mascarille; but as he grew older he began to write plays in which the chief part was that of the middle-aged man, usually the father, and the role of helper of the young lovers was passed to an outspoken female servant. (Figure 2, a fine baroque design, shows Molière in his early roles as Mascarille – here disguised as a *marquis* – and Sganarelle.)

In the original, stock plot the father is simply a blocking character, with little individuality: he is often simply given the name of Géronte (old man). The middle-aged men played by Molière are much more interesting. The first is Arnolphe in *L'Ecole des femmes* (1661), a *bourgeois* who has decided to marry his own seventeen-year-old ward: his scheme is frustrated, in a pleasing variation on the usual pattern, by a naive young man and two deeply stupid servants, and also the naive but far from stupid girl herself. The action is set, not in Sicily or Spain, but in a recognizably contemporary small French town. The play had a *succès de scandale* due to its light-hearted approach to the theme of female virtue. But *Tartuffe* was to give much more serious offence. Again, it is a family drama set in a prosperous bourgeois household, but this time the lovers' future is threatened by the father Orgon's new obsession with religion. He has fallen under the influence of a pious layman, Tartuffe, who undertakes to reform the household, much to the disgust of Dorine, the female upper servant. Orgon so admires Tartuffe that he has decided to leave him all his money, and has already made over the house to him; he also means to give Tartuffe his daughter's hand in marriage, although he had previously agreed her engagement to someone else. Meanwhile, Tartuffe is planning to seduce Orgon's wife Elmire.

The choice of this subject was bound to be dangerous. Convention did not allow religious practices to be shown or even mentioned on the stage (even the word '*église*' (church) was usually replaced by 'temple' in play scripts). So when Orgon describes the ostentatious prayers by which Tartuffe first attracted his attention 'à l'église' (Act I, scene 5), or when Tartuffe makes his first appearance fresh from mortifying the flesh (III, 2) and proceeds to make advances to Elmire using the language of mysticism (III, 3) many in the audience will have been genuinely shocked. The young, pleasure-loving king and his contemporaries no doubt enjoyed the play, with its frank attacks on prudery and hypocrisy (see Text 4), but the older circle around the Queen Mother, and the representatives of the Church attached to the court, were outraged, and prevailed upon the king to forbid public performance of the play until further notice. Clearly Molière was attached to the play more than can be explained simply by the wish not to lose the investment any play represented in writing and rehearsal time. He continued battling for the right to put it on, attempted more than one rewrite and eventually got his wish in 1669. The text we have is certainly not identical to the one first staged in 1664, which is lost, but it is recognizably the same play. Historically it has been his most successful, and is still often staged today.

TEXT 4 A HYPOCRITE REVEALED

Tartuffe, the name-character of the play, does not actually appear on stage until this point, at the beginning of Act III, scene 2. But we have heard a great deal about him already, from Act I scene 1 onwards. In the eyes of Orgon, the master of the house, he is a holy man, but the terms in which Orgon praises him (Act I, scene 5) have already made us suspicious. Dorine, the outspoken female servant, regards him as simply a fraud, with his eyes on Orgon's money and his attractive wife. Here we are finally allowed to judge for ourselves. Tartuffe's first lines, spoken to his servant offstage, are prompted by the appearance of Dorine. (What was he doing before he saw her?) Her first line is no doubt an aside.

TARTUFFE, *apercevant Dorine*
Laurent, serrez ma haire avec ma discipline
Et priez que toujours le Ciel vous illumine.
Si l'on vient pour me voir, je vais aux prisonniers
Des aumônes que j'ai partager les deniers.

DORINE
Que d'affectation et de forfanterie!

TARTUFFE
Que voulez-vous?

DORINE
Vous dire ...

TARTUFFE. *Il tire un mouchoir de sa poche.*
Ah! mon Dieu, je vous prie.
Avant que de parler prenez-moi ce mouchoir.

DORINE
Comment?

TARTUFFE
Couvrez ce sein que je ne saurais voir:
Par de pareils objets les âmes sont blessées,
Et cela fait venir de coupables pensées.

DORINE
Vous êtes donc bien tendre à la tentation,
Et la chair sur vos sens fait grande impression!
Certes, je ne sais pas quelle chaleur vous monte:
Mais à convoiter, moi, je ne suis point si prompte,
Et je vous verrais nu du haut jusques en bas
Que toute votre peau ne me tenterait pas.

TARTUFFE
Mettez dans vos discours un peu de modestie
Ou je vais sur-le-champ vous quitter la partie.

DORINE
Non, non, c'est moi qui vais vous laisser en repos,
Et je n'ai seulement qu'à vous dire deux mots.
Madame va venir dans cette salle basse,
Et d'un mot d'entretien vous demande la grâce.

TARTUFFE
Hélas! très volontiers.

DORINE, *en soi-même*
Comme il se radoucit!
Ma foi, je suis toujours pour ce que j'en ai dit.

[TARTUFFE (*noticing Dorine*): Laurent, you can put away my hair-
    shirt and my scourge now, and pray Heaven to give you grace.

If anyone calls for me, I'll be visiting the prisoners, sharing what alms I have with them.

DORINE: Listen to him! What a show-off!

TARTUFFE: What do you want?

DORINE: Just to tell you ...

TARTUFFE (*producing a handkerchief*) Oh! For Heaven's sake, before you speak, take this handkerchief.

DORINE: What?

TARTUFFE: Cover that bosom, I will not look at it. Such sights are dangerous to souls: they make us have shameful thoughts.

DORINE: Well, you're very subject to temptation I must say, and flesh makes a great impression on your senses! I don't know what your trouble is, but I'm not so easily led astray: I could see you naked from head to foot and the whole of your skin wouldn't tempt me in the least.

TARTUFFE: Speak more modestly, please, or I shall have to leave you.

DORINE: No, no, I'll be leaving *you* in peace: I just have one thing to tell you. The mistress is coming down and would like a word with you.

TARTUFFE: Why, of course!

DORINE (*aside*): Suddenly he's all sweetness! I bet I was right in what I said just now.]

By the time *Tartuffe* (now called *Le Tartuffe, ou l'Imposteur*) finally received public staging, Molière had written, produced and appeared in a further nine plays, many of them *comédies-ballets*, entertainments premiered at court (and produced there with a lavishness impossible to copy today) and then put on in reduced versions at Molière's Paris theatre. He was to go on creating these fanciful musical pieces, often with a spoken prose text at the heart of them, for the rest of his life. At the same time he was writing bourgeois family comedies for his town theatre, with himself as the self-centred father: *L'Avare, Les Femmes savantes*. His two most memorable and best-loved late plays combine the family comedy in a bourgeois setting with improbable schemes of self-transformation by the father: *Le Bourgeois gentilhomme* (The Middle-Class Nobleman) and *Le Malade imaginaire* (The Imaginary Invalid). Both were musical plays, premiered at court (the sung and danced parts originally considerably longer than the spoken play) and each ends in a ballet that embraces the father's folly and seems to transport it to a higher plane of blissful release from everyday common sense. It was while singing and clowning in the final musical number of *Le Malade imaginaire* on 17 February 1673 that Molière collapsed, was carried home and died that evening (probably of tuberculosis) without the sacraments, to the ill-concealed delight of his clerical adversaries. His wife had the greatest difficulty in getting him buried in consecrated ground. After his death, the king forced an amalgamation of his troupe with the other stable acting company in the capital, to form the Comédie-Française or, as it is still familiarly called, 'la maison de Molière'.

Of all his plays, perhaps the most interesting – at any rate, the most original – is *Le Misanthrope* (1666), which departs from the family-comedy formula since all its characters are of similar age, live independently in Paris and can decide on their own relationships. At sea in this modern world is Alceste, Molière's character, who expects to be able to live like a nobleman of former times rather than jockey for preferment at court, and tries to exercise an almost fatherly authority over the heroine, Célimène, a widow of twenty who is determined to keep her independence.

Molière is the author whom almost every Frenchman and woman has encountered, if only at school. In journalistic writing, French is still referred to as 'la langue de Molière'; English is 'la langue de Shakespeare'. Like Shakespeare, Molière did not trouble to publish all his plays in his lifetime; the collected edition produced by members of his company after his death includes thirty-four titles. In France his plays are still constantly performed in commercial as well as subsidized theatres.

Racine

Whereas Molière lived and, one might say, died for the theatre, **Jean Racine** (1639–99) wrote for it only during the years 1664–77. During that time he wrote nine tragedies and one comedy. He never acted nor directed: his relationship to the acting companies was the traditional one of *poète* (supplier of scripts), but not *à gages*.

The son of a legal family, Racine was educated at Port-Royal, a sternly pious foundation, and was originally intended for the church. He did take minor orders but did not proceed to full ordination, which meant that he was later free to marry. Around the age of twenty he moved to Paris and, to the alarm of his family and schoolmasters, began to frequent the literary and theatrical worlds. His first tragedies were given to Molière's company, who were known for their more modern and realistic acting style. However when they had already learned and rehearsed the second of these, *Alexandre le grand* (1665), Racine transferred it to the more traditional and highly regarded Hôtel de Bourgogne troupe, causing a lasting split between the two great dramatists. All of Racine's remaining secular tragedies were staged at the Hôtel de Bourgogne, where he promoted himself as the youthful rival and replacement of the aging Corneille: mostly with success. *Phèdre* (1677), now considered his greatest tragedy, was not so successful as some of the others.

At this point he abandoned the commercial theatre, made a respectable marriage, was reconciled to Port-Royal and accepted the appointment of historiographer-royal along with his friend Boileau. This post, which involved travelling with the king on his progresses and campaigns, was obviously regarded as much more honourable than writing for the theatre. A decade later, however, when the king had secretly married the last of his mistresses, Madame de Maintenon, and that lady had somewhat improbably brought him back to a life of greater piety and tried to reform the tone of the court, Racine accepted commissions from her to write two plays for the young ladies to perform at the school she had founded for them, Saint-Cyr. These two plays on Biblical subjects, *Esther* (1689) and *Athalie* (1691), are naturally rather different from the tragedies Racine had written for the commercial stage. For one thing, they include musical interludes (to allow the young ladies to show off their vocal and instrumental accomplishments, no doubt). More importantly, the driving force in all of Racine's secular tragedies is sexual passion: a theme to be avoided at all costs in a play for a girls' school.

Love plays little part if any in ancient tragedy: ancient Greek plays were written by men to be performed by men before an audience made up almost entirely of men. The themes that interested them were honour, conflict, fate and above all the relationship of human beings to the gods. By Corneille's time the supernatural side of tragedy had been allowed to lapse, and young heroes might be in love and be motivated by love, even if the old warriors dismissed it: 'Nous n'avons qu'un honneur, il est tant de maîtresses', says Rodrigue's father in *Le Cid*. (We have only one honour, girlfriends are a dime a dozen). No one in a Racine tragedy is allowed to talk like this. The love interest is now everything. As **Nicolas Boileau-Despréaux** (1636–1711), Racine's friend, put it in his potted history of tragedy in Canto III of *L'Art poétique* (1674):

> Bientôt l'amour, fertile en tendres sentiments
> S'empara du théâtre, ainsi que des romans.
> De cette passion la sensible peinture
> Est pour aller au cœur la route la plûs sure.
> Peignez donc, j'y consens, les héros amoureux ...

> [Soon love, a fertile source of tender feelings
> Took over the stage as it had novels.
> Vivid portrayal of this passion
> Is the quickest way to the audience's heart.
> So show your heroes in love, I permit it ...]

This sounds grudging ('j'y consens'), and it is immediately followed by a 'but':

> Mais ne m'en formez point des bergers doucereux

> [But don't turn them into sugar-tongued shepherds
> (like the shepherds of pastoral)].

Boileau was a traditionalist. But most commentators by Racine's time agree that any tragedy without a love interest is doomed to failure. Love is the mainspring of all Racine's plots, but there is rarely anything 'doucereux' about it: it is savage. Pyrrhus in *Andromaque* (1667, Racine's first big success) tries to force Andromaque's consent to marriage by threatening to hand her son over to the Greeks, who will kill him; meanwhile Hermione, betrothed to Pyrrhus who now scorns her (see Text 5), tricks Oreste, who loves her, into murdering Pyrrhus and then rejects him, literally driving him mad. In *Britannicus* (1669) the emperor Nero is so jealous of Junie's love for his half-brother Britannicus that he has him murdered, and the end of the play looks forward to his murder of the mother they share, the empress Agrippina. In *Bajazet* (1672, set in near-contemporary Turkey) the dominant character, who can command everything but love, is a woman, the favourite concubine given temporary control of the palace, Roxane. When Bajazet will not love her she sends him to be strangled, but her own death soon follows, and the girl Bajazet did love takes her own life. *Bérénice* (1670) and *Mithridate* (1673) are gentler, the latter having an almost happy ending. But there is still nothing saccharine about their treatment of passion.

TEXT 5 A WOMAN SCORNED
(RACINE, *ANDROMAQUE*, ACT IV, SCENE 6)

Hermione, a Spartan princess, was promised in marriage to Pyrrhus, king of Epirus and has already made the sea journey to Epirus for the wedding. But Pyrrhus now loves Andromaque, widow of Hector, and is trying to find excuses for abandoning Hermione. Here he argues that theirs was only a dynastic betrothal, arranged by their parents: perhaps Hermione will be glad to be freed from it. Up to this point she has been calling him 'vous', in the polite fashion befitting a princess. But at line 1356, overcome by anger and frustrated love, she shifts to 'tu'. At line 1369 she will regain control and revert to 'vous'.

PYRRHUS
Nos cœurs n'étaient point faits dépendants l'un de l'autre
Je suivais mon devoir, et vous cédiez au vôtre :
Rien ne vous engageait à m'aimer en effet.   1355

HERMIONE
Je ne t'ai point aimé, cruel ! Qu'ai-je donc fait ?
J'ai dédaigné pour toi les vœux de tous nos princes,
Je t'ai cherché moi-même au fond de tes provinces.

J'y suis encore, malgré tes infidélités,
Et malgré tous mes Grecs honteux de mes bontés.   1360
Je leur ai commandé de cacher mon injure ;
J'attendais en secret le retour d'un parjure ;
J'ai cru que tôt ou tard, à ton devoir rendu,
Tu me rapporterais un cœur qui m'était dû.
Je t'aimais inconstant, qu'aurais-je fait fidèle?   1365
Et même en ce moment, où ta bouche cruelle
Vient si tranquillement m'annoncer le trépas,
Ingrat, je doute encore si je ne t'aime pas.

[Pyrrhus: Our hearts were not made dependent one on the other.
I was following my duty, and you were submitting to yours. Nothing
committed you to loving me in reality.

Hermione: I haven't loved you! What have I done, then? For you
I refused the suit of all the Greek princes; I came myself to join you
in your far-off province. I'm still here, in spite of your unfaithful-
ness, and in spite of my Greek escort, who are all ashamed of my
tolerance of you. I have ordered them to keep the insult to me
hidden; I was waiting in secret for a traitor's return. I thought
that sooner or later, returning to your duty, you would bring me a
heart that was mine by right. I loved you inconstant: faithful, what
would I have done? And at this very moment, when your cruel lips
come so calmly to announce my death, ungrateful wretch, I cannot
be sure I do not love you still.]

Even when Racine adapted his play from a Greek source, which
he did in *Iphigénie* (1674) and *Phèdre* (1677), he felt obliged to
develop a love plot by introducing new characters and heavily
modifying some of the original ones. In the original story of
Phaedra, the goddess Aphrodite punished the young queen for a
crime committed by her ancestors by inflicting upon her an
intense sexual passion for her stepson, the chaste prince Hippolytus,
who wished only to have nothing to do with women. Such a
character would have had little appeal to the contemporaries of

Louis XIV. So Racine introduces the new character of Aricie, an equally chaste princess for whom Hippolyte can fall, experiencing love for the first time. The noble shared feelings of these youthful characters are contrasted with the guilty passion of the queen, which horrifies her as much as anyone: 'une passion dont elle a horreur toute la première', says Racine in his preface to the play (a passion that she is the first to reject with horror). But the working-out of the gods' curse costs the lives of both Hippolyte and Phèdre, who poisons herself in the last scene.

In Corneille love is often seen as an ennobling emotion that inspires heroes to great deeds: in Racine it appears more like an illness, an irresistible drive propelling people towards actions that appal even themselves. The sufferers from this *amour-passion* are very often women, princesses or queens as the dignity of tragedy requires; most of the best roles in Racine are for actresses. They were played first by La Duparc, then, after her death in 1668, by La Champmeslé, who created the roles of Bérénice, Roxane, Monime (in *Mithridate*) and Phèdre. Racine was supposed to have been the lover of both women, and to have coached La Champmeslé in the speaking of his verse.

Compared to the rolling declamation required by Corneille, Racine's lines seem quiet. He employs an even smaller vocabulary than Corneille's: about 3,000 words (compare Shakespeare's 30,000), from which everything extreme, far-fetched or gory has been expunged. It is the contrast between the desperate passions and bloody deeds of his characters and the melodious, almost polite language in which they are expressed that is so striking.

Prose and non-dramatic verse

The seventeenth century saw the development of systematic philosophical and scientific writing in French. Two great mathematicians, **René Descartes** (1596–1650), the inventor of Cartesian or analytical geometry, and **Blaise Pascal** (1623–62), of triangle fame, are also important figures in the history of French literature. Descartes wrote mostly in Latin, still the main international language of intellectual exchange, but his *Discours de la méthode,* published in 1637 in French to introduce his ideas to laymen and women, had great influence. His reasoning method was initially to set aside as uncertain anything of which he could not be absolutely sure. He was left only with the realisation that 'je pense, donc je suis' (in Latin, *cogito, ergo sum*, I think (or rather: 'I am – now – thinking'), therefore I am). Having thus established the fact of his own existence, he proceeds by purely logical deduction to re-establish the existence and goodness of God, the existence of material objects and indeed most of the propositions he had set aside in the first chapter. But they are now worthy of belief because they have been established by reason, if possible, by mathematical reasoning. Much later in life, Descartes produced another work in French, the *Traité des passions de l'âme* (1649), in which he systematically analyses the full range of human feelings (such things as envy, fear or shame can be classed as 'passions' in this use of the word, since they are things that the soul 'undergoes') and shows how they can be brought under control by the use, again, of reason. Frenchmen have traditionally prided themselves on the nation's 'esprit cartésien', its natural preference for reason and logic over emotion.

Whether or not this is justified, it is not a claim that Pascal would have made for himself. Though he admired the older man as a mathematician, Pascal, the son of an austerely pious family of the lawyer/civil servant class and himself, in his later life, of a piety bordering on mysticism, thought Descartes' reliance on pure reason blasphemous. Mere human reasoning could not bridge the gap between man and God. For that the gift of faith was required – a free gift from God that could be prayed for but not compelled. This is obviously an idea akin to Protestantism;

in France at this time it was associated with the Catholic group called (by others) Jansenists, centred at Port-Royal.

As well as his scientific work, Pascal left two substantial pieces of writing in French. The first of these, the *Lettres provinciales* (1656–67), is a collection of satirical letters written in the character of a somewhat naive provincial gentleman reporting to a friend at home on the doctrinal disputes then raging between the Jansenists and the Jesuits, who enjoyed much greater favour at court. Behind the letter-writer's initially naive accounts, Pascal lets us see the Jesuits' worldliness and lax moral teaching, which become clearer and inspire the writer to increasing anger as the letters progress.

Despite their now remote subject, the *Lettres* are still worth reading for their wit and trenchant style. Later in life, however, Pascal reproached himself for having written them: wit was never an appropriate mode in writing about sacred subjects. Instead he began to make notes for a more complete and effective defence of Christian belief: an apologia. He died long before this was complete, leaving a mountain of notes on small slips of paper: his friends at Port-Royal took on the task of turning this into a publishable work, but did not feel they could give it any title but *Pensées de M. Pascal sur divers sujets* (Thoughts of M. Pascal upon various subjects, 1670). Successive editors from then until now have put the book together again in a variety of shapes. The only thing that seems constant is that it was to have been in two parts, 'Misère de l'homme sans Dieu' and 'Félicité de l'homme avec Dieu' (Man's misery without God and happiness with him); the first was much nearer completion on Pascal's death. Instead of proceeding, like Descartes or a medieval apologist, from first principles and demonstrating first the existence and then the goodness of God, Pascal starts with man and shows his weakness, inability to achieve sure knowledge and aching need for a higher being on whom to rely. This will be the Romantic and twentieth-century approach to belief, which has ensured that the

Pensées have continued to be widely read and admired in modern times.

In dwelling on the 'misère de l'homme sans Dieu', Pascal resembles other contemporary writers who are generally grouped together under the title 'les moralistes'. The name means not 'moralisers', but students of the psychological (as opposed to physical) aspects of man. **François, duc de La Rochefoucauld** (1613–80) was the author of a book of *Maximes* first published in 1665 and then in many subsequent editions, each bringing additional material. The fragmentary form of the *Maximes,* unlike that of the *Pensées*, is entirely deliberate: many are only one sentence long. They express a disillusioned but penetrating view of human behaviour, whether in social or love relationships, or even in man's relation to himself.

La Rochefoucauld is supposed to have developed his world-view, and honed his style, in the salons of ladies like Mme de Sévigné (**Marie de Rabutin-Chantal, marquise de Sévigné**, 1626–96, famous for her letters published after her death), Mme de Sablé and Mme de Lafayette, whom we shall presently encounter as a novelist.

The other celebrated 'moraliste' is **Jean de la Bruyère** (1645–96). Born into the lesser nobility (the *noblesse de robe*), he came to court as tutor to the son of one of the most powerful of the great nobles, the Prince de Condé. This meant that he could observe Versailles from within, but always as an outsider. His *Caractères* (1688) depict the life of the town, the court and the literary world, with reflections on women, love and fortune. Almost all the items are short, anything from a sentence to a couple of pages: the mean length is a paragraph or two. His style is much more varied than La Rochefoucauld's and he includes picturesque detail, which the duke entirely omits.

The development of the novel in the reigns of Louis XIII and Louis XIV is usually linked to growing freedom for the women of the higher classes, and the development of the *salon* as a social institution. The *salon* was a regular gathering of friends in the house of a woman, usually but not necessarily married. Time might be spent simply in gossip and chat, but in certain salons the discussion became more systematic and the topics more serious, including literature and the development of the language. The inexhaustible topic, however, was love: how a lover should behave to his lady, what familiarities if any she could allow him, the characters of individual lovers and ladies, how love might be depicted in literature, what kind of language was precise and yet decent enough to express the various stages of a love affair. There would have been music, the recitation of impromptu poems and readings from works in progress. Men as well as women attended these gatherings, but power clearly resided with the hostess and her closest friends: a power that they did not enjoy anywhere outside the home. The salon was therefore a tiny oasis of sex equality in a very unequal society. The first recorded salons of this kind were those of the Marquise de Rambouillet, from about 1620 to 1650, and of **Madeleine de Scudéry** (1607–1701), a well-educated bourgeoise, in the 1640s and 1650s. This latter lady was the author of various novels published under her brother's name, of which the most successful were *Le Grand Cyrus* and *Clélie*. They are long, rambling, multi-volume adventure stories, tales of ill-starred love in which the hero, often disguised, must seek his beloved over continents and years, only to find her in the end as beautiful and virginal as ever. Not only do the heroes appear disguised in the narrative (Cyrus of Persia under the name Artamène, for example), but Cyrus/Artamène and the other characters are also, it appears, thinly disguised versions of well-known contemporaries, who are constantly interrupting the action to sit down and hold the same long discussions about the passion and morality of love that they might have held in Mlle de Scudéry's own salon. Hugely successful at the time (they were soon translated into English and avidly read by, for example, Mrs Samuel Pepys), these novels are quite unreadable today.

The guests of Mme de Rambouillet and readers of Mlle de Scudéry were given (by others) the name of 'précieuses' and were cruelly satirised by male authors including Molière (*Les Précieuses ridicules*, 1659) and Boileau (*Dialogue des héros de roman,* written 1665, published 1714). But the 'heroic novel', as these far-fetched affairs are called, continued to be written and read well into the eighteenth century: Voltaire's *Candide* (1759) is, among other things, a parody of this type of book.

Much more acceptable to modern readers is the kind of novel written, and published anonymously, by a later and more aristocratic salon hostess, **Madame de Lafayette** (1634–92). Her novels are short, and, apart from one with a Turkish setting, located in France, never far from the court, and in relatively recent times. Her masterpiece, *La Princesse de Clèves* (1678) is set around the year 1559, but her picture of court life then owes much to her own experience of the court of Louis XIV. At the centre of each of her novels is a young woman of the aristocracy, whose experience of life and love is set out in a very restrained style, but with great psychological penetration. Especially in contrast to the 'heroic' novel, Madame de Lafayette's may be described as realistic, though of course they are not at all like the realist novels of the nineteenth century.

Many letters and memoirs of court life from this period were published, usually after their authors' deaths. Madame de Lafayette left an *Histoire de Madame Henriette d'Angleterre,* the king's sister-in-law who had been her friend and had died unexpectedly in 1670, and two memoirs of the court for 1688 and 1689, eventually published in 1734. Lively accounts of the earlier part of Louis XIV's reign can be found in the memoirs of **Paul de Gondi, Cardinal de Retz** (1614–79), of the latter part in the letters (translated from German) of **Elizabeth-Charlotte de Bavière, Princesse Palatine**, who succeeded Henriette d'Angleterre as the king's sister-in-law, and in the memoirs of **Louis de Rouvroy, duc de Saint-Simon** (1675–1755).

The lyric poetry of this period is an acquired taste: affected by the 'précieux' spirit, it tends to be conventional and somewhat insipid. Boileau's rhymed satires can be trenchant in the Roman satiric mode, but apart from verse written for the stage, the only seventeenth-century poetry most French people know is a handful of the *Fables* of **Jean de La Fontaine,** which they probably learned by heart at school. These masterly short pieces, with their light, irregular rhythms, have traditionally been considered suitable for children, though the morals they draw are often disillusioned if not grim (rather like Lewis Carroll's parodies in *Alice in Wonderland*).

TEXT 6 THE CICADA AND THE ANT

This is the first (Book I, 1) of La Fontaine's *Fables*, which eventually grew to fill twelve books. The first volume, containing Books 1–6, was published in 1668 and dedicated to the seven-year-old son and heir of Louis XIV. French children have been learning them by heart ever since (the little daughter of Molière's *Malade imaginaire*, 1673, offers to recite one, Act II sc 8), and many adults can still recall this example. The last line somehow seems quintessentially French.

La cigale, ayant chanté
        Tout l'été
Se trouva fort dépourvue
Quand la bise fut venue.
Pas un seul petit morceau
De mouche ou de vermisseau.
Elle alla crier famine
Chez la fourmi sa voisine,
La priant de lui prêter
Quelque grain pour subsister
Jusqu'à la saison nouvelle.
'Je vous paierai, lui dit-elle,

Avant l'août, foi d'animal,
Intérêt et principal'.
La fourmi n'est point prêteuse ;
C'est là son moindre défaut.
'Que faisiez-vous au temps chaud ?'
Dit-elle à cette emprunteuse.
– Nuit et jour à tout venant
– Je chantais, ne vous déplaise.
– Vous chantiez ? J'en suis fort aise.
Eh bien ! Dansez maintenant'.

[The cicada, having sung all the summer, found herself ill provided for when the cold winds came. Not even a scrap of fly or worm. She went to plead poverty at the house of her neighbour the ant, begging her for the loan of a few grains to survive until the new season. 'I'll pay you back', she said, 'before August, animal's honour, principal and interest'. The ant is not a lender: that's the fault she's least subject to. 'What were you doing in the hot weather?', she asked the would-be borrower. 'Night and day I sang to all comers, if you please'. 'You sang? That's nice. Well, you can dance now'].

Rousseau, an inveterate borrower himself, says in his *Emile* (1762, see text 8), that children should not learn anything by heart, not even fables and particularly not this one – 'Quelle horrible leçon pour l'enfance'.

The baroque

When French literature began to be taught in schools and universities, a canon was quickly established in which the 'grands classiques' of the seventeenth century were the chief models for imitation. The word 'classiques' originally meant simply 'the texts taught in classes'. Writers like Molière and Racine would never have thought of themselves as 'classiques', since the writers they studied in their classes were Latin and Greek. But teachers soon recognized in these approved writers a set of characteristics which they called 'classicisme': logic, restraint, understatement, linguistic purity. Writers lacking these qualities were excluded from the canon. The nineteenth-century Romantics defined themselves against these qualities, and some of them, notably Hugo, were in due course admitted to the school canon. But the seventeenth century, the *grand siècle*, was still seen as the century of classicism. From about 1950 this prejudice began to be questioned, and a series of writers overlooked since their own day came to be read and appreciated again, rather as the metaphysical poets came to be admired again in England and America in the 1920s. These once-excluded, now-admired writers were given the name of 'baroques', a term whose only meaning in the seventeenth century had been 'misshapen', as applied to pearls. Art historians had already applied it to painting (e.g. Rubens) or architecture (e.g. Bernini) and it was felt that the 'baroque' writers shared some of the characteristics of these artists (extravagance, theatricality, deliberate confusions between the real and the artificial). The baroque form *par excellence* was the theatre, and within that the opera, which became increasingly appreciated in the late seventeenth century. Extremely expensive to stage, opera was at this time essentially a court entertainment. A late-seventeenth-century opera was a collaboration of all the arts: poetry, singing, orchestral music, but also dancing and elaborate stage effects – lavish built and painted sets, transformation scenes, flying chariots and the like. Much of this expertise was imported from Italy: the king of opera composers was **Jean-Baptiste Lully** (born Giovanbattista Lulli in Florence in 1632, died in Paris at the height of his power in 1687), and the prince of stage designers **Carlo Vigarani** (1637–1713), 'intendant des plaisirs du roi' of Louis XIV, whose father had overseen the building of the 'Salle des Machines' theatre at the Tuileries palace and who in his turn masterminded the 'Plaisirs de î'Ile enchantée' at Versailles mentioned above, the very model of a baroque entertainment. Now that 'baroque' writing has, albeit tentatively, re-entered the canon, people are beginning to see baroque elements even in the 'grands classiques'. An unquestionable example would be the 'tragédie-comédie-ballet' *Psyché* of 1671 (the very mixture would now be considered 'baroque'), a court entertainment with book by Molière and Corneille and lyrics by Quinault, music by Lully and sets by Carlo Vigarani. As well as some genuinely moving poetry and enchanting music, it includes what is probably the stage prototype of the 'two ugly sisters', as well as extravagant palace and garden sets (two full transformations), much flying (Venus's chariot had to be big enough to carry four people) and an interlude set in Hell with eye-catching machinery and dancing demons.

It is easy to think of seventeenth-century literature in terms of public performance, official and grandiose, but the great writers' over-riding interest in human feelings and behaviour can be just as well expressed in studies of the individual in his or her private world.

4

The eighteenth century: the Republic of Letters

In 1715 Louis XIV died after a reign lasting seventy-two years, still the longest of any European monarch. He was succeeded by his five-year-old great-grandson, all intervening heirs having predeceased the old king (killed off, some said, by the most expensive doctors in the kingdom). This inevitably meant another regency. The regent this time was Philippe d'Orléans, the king's nephew, son of La Palatine, a highly intelligent but dissipated man who took up residence away from the gloom of Versailles in the Palais-Royal in Paris. This move was marked by a change in intellectual and moral atmosphere: intellectual curiosity, scepticism and frivolity were once more welcome at court.

The young king began his official reign in 1723, aged thirteen, and occupied the throne until his death in 1774, ruling from Versailles with the help of a succession of ministers and other powers behind the throne, including, notably, the Marquise de Pompadour, who was his mistress in the 1740s but continued as a friend and adviser until her death in 1764.

Politically and militarily Louis' reign was a period of decline for France: she lost her colonies in Canada and India, and the combined costs of foreign wars and the upkeep of the court required constant tax increases that infuriated the public. As nobles and churchmen were exempt from taxes, the costs fell on the so-called Third Estate, that is, everyone else, and in practice largely on the middle classes, though even the poor felt the weight of duties on such necessaries as salt and wine, and the country poor owed feudal taxes and labour duties to their land-lords. Despite these dissatisfactions, the same period was the one in which French intellectual and artistic influence in and beyond Europe was perhaps the greatest. It was at this time that French became the language of diplomacy and of polite conversation among the upper classes in most of the European states and as far afield as Russia. The most important writers did not simply serve the court but were based in Paris, finding their patrons among the aristocracy, who were building themselves grand new town houses (*hôtels*) in the Saint-Germain district, or among the *grands bourgeois*, some of whom were now extremely rich, having made their fortunes in tax-gathering or finance or, for some of them, in trade, entrepreneurship and invention.

Many members of the Third Estate became increasingly intolerant of the inferior social status officially imposed on them, and questioned the privileges enjoyed by aristocrats simply by virtue of their birth. In an angry monologue, Figaro, the clever servant in Beaumarchais' play *Le Mariage de Figaro,* lists all the advantages the count enjoys, and asks his absent master, 'What did you do to deserve all this? Vous vous êtes donné la peine de naître, et rien de plus.' (You took the trouble to be born, nothing more).

In 1774 Louis XV was succeeded by his grandson, the some-what lacklustre Louis XVI, under whom and his wife, the lively but ill-advised Austrian princess Marie-Antoinette, the court became ever more extravagant and (certainly not for this reason alone) the economic situation of the country more desperate. All of these factors – bourgeois resentment, desperation of the poor, interest in republican ideas among intellectuals, encouraged by the example of the American revolution of 1776 – came together to produce the revolution which started in 1789 but took three years to bring about the end of the monarchy and a further year to see the execution first of the king and later of the queen.

The intellectually curious living in the same city could also exchange their ideas at meetings of learned societies created for the purpose: in London the Royal Society or Society of Antiquaries, in Paris the various Académies. But at least as important in Paris were salons, informal but regular meetings in private houses. Like the seventeenth-century salons these were typically hosted by ladies, and no doubt a good deal went on there that was not particularly serious: gossip, cards, music, flirtation. But new ideas in literature, philosophy, science and politics were also discussed in the salons, and groups formed to carry these ideas forward.

All of the writers the French call the *philosophes* frequented such gatherings, and so learned to formulate their ideas in language that ladies and gentlemen, and not just scholars, could understand. An early and striking example of this method is the *Entretiens sur la pluralité des mondes habités* (Discussions about the plurality of inhabited worlds, 1686) by **Bernard le Bovier de Fontenelle** (1657–1757), a corresponding member of the Royal Society of London who became secretaire Perpétual of the Paris Académie des Sciences in 1697, and lived up to the title by serving for a further sixty years. The *Entretiens* are a series of lively, almost flirtatious conversations between the narrator and a *marquise* about the possibility of life on other planets, in the course of which he manages to impart a good deal of information about the structure of the cosmos and the scientific method of inquiry.

Voltaire

Voltaire (1694–1778) is taken as the embodiment of French literature in the eighteenth century as Victor Hugo was in the nineteenth, and for some of the same reasons. Both began writing and publishing very young and continued into old age, so that each left a very large output. Each spoke out against oppression and in favour of 'progressive' values, thus earning censorship, legal condemnation and exile, though both returned to France in old age to public acclaim. But otherwise they are very different. Hugo made most of his effects by appealing to the emotions, using broad, sweeping rhetoric, whereas Voltaire is usually light and sprightly and always at least pretends to be appealing to reason, though he is a master of biased presentation, irony and humour.

Voltaire was born François-Marie Arouet *le jeune* (the younger), to a prosperous legal family, and was educated in the same Jesuit school as Molière, though its name had now been changed to the Collège Louis-le-Grand. As a schoolboy he frequented freethinking *milieux*, and a daring political lampoon landed him in the Bastille for eleven months. He used the time to write his first tragedy, *Oedipe*, and to work on an epic poem with Henri IV as its hero, later published as *La Henriade*. These he published under the pseudonym Voltaire, thought to be an anagram of Arouet l.j. (AROVET L I in Latin characters), a name which he kept for the rest of his life and made famous throughout Europe. Despite his bourgeois origins his wit allowed him to move in the highest social circles, until he risked a public quarrel with a member of one of the grandest families, the chevalier de Rohan, and found himself in the Bastille again. On his release he took refuge in England, where he remained for three years: his friends there came to include Congreve, Berkeley, Bolingbroke, Pope and Swift.

His time in England inspired a short set of letters published as the *Lettres philosophiques* or *Lettres sur les Anglais* (1734), contrasting English and French customs. Rather like Pascal in the *Lettres provinciales*, which he much admired, Voltaire writes in the character of a travelling Frenchman who has little understanding of English values. But it is plain that Voltaire himself embraced them warmly. He particularly admired England's constitutional (as opposed to France's absolute) monarchy, and the religious toleration that allowed Englishmen of different observances to live in peace with each other. The work was promptly condemned and ordered to be burnt by the public hangman, and the author to be arrested. Voltaire fled Paris and lived for the next ten years at the house of his mistress Madame du Châtelet (a self-funding scientist in her own right) at Cirey, near the border with Lorraine, over which he could escape if necessary.

After 1744 he was able to return to Paris and even to go to court, where he was supported by Madame de Pompadour despite the king's mistrust, and to rebuild his reputation as a writer of tragedies. Still he never felt secure, and after Madame du Châtelet died he accepted the invitation of Frederick II of Prussia to live and work at his palace in Potsdam. Two such large egos could not easily live together, and after three years Voltaire moved to Switzerland, where he bought a country house. But his relations with the Calvinists of Geneva were no better than they had been with the Catholics of Paris, and he eventually settled at Ferney, just on the French side of the border, allowing for escape in either direction according to circumstances. In this situation of apparent instability he constructed the most stable life he had ever enjoyed. Clever investment had made him rich, and he was able to buy a large estate where he lived the life of a model improving landlord while constantly writing, publishing (often anonymously or under pseudonyms) and corresponding with members of the République des lettres throughout Europe (his collected letters fill some fifteen thousand printed pages). He lived at Ferney for eighteen years, returning to Paris for the staging of his last tragedy, *Irène* (1778), which was a triumph: he was crowned with a laurel wreath by the ecstatic audience of the Odéon. But he was already ill, and died in Paris some weeks later.

Voltaire's surviving work includes dozens of plays, mostly tragedies (successful in their day but never revived now), poems, epic and didactic as well as lyric, histories of Louis XIV and Charles XII of Sweden, letters and dialogues and countless short satirical and polemical publications, many of which he disowned but which were nonetheless recognizably his. He is now chiefly remembered for his twelve 'contes philosophiques', tales exploring epistemological and moral puzzles. Some of these were written in midlife (*Zadig*, 1747; *Micromégas,* a kind of early science-fiction story, 1739–52), but the greatest, *Candide* (1759) and *L'Ingénu* (1767), when he was already old. The second is really more of a short novel. It is the story of a young man, at first believed to be a Huron, a Native Canadian, shipwrecked on the shore of Brittany, but who turns out to be (rather like Tarzan) the orphan child of a couple of French colonists, brought up by the Hurons. The first chapters are broadly comical, as *l'Ingénu* (The Innocent) tries to understand French ideas and master French manners, which Voltaire takes the opportunity of mocking. But when the boy falls in love with a French girl the story turns more sentimental. She is taken from him and he has to pursue her to Versailles: cue for an angrily satirical portrait of the life of a petitioner at court. The girl, Mademoiselle de Saint-Yves, sacrifices her honour for her lover's freedom and dies of shame, leaving a wiser but much sadder *Ingénu* to gain military glory in the army of Louis XIV.

Candide is shorter and more unified: most people consider it Voltaire's masterpiece. On the level of plot, it is a parody of the 'heroic novel' described in our previous chapter, made comical first of all by its extreme concision (one slim volume instead of ten fat ones). The hero and heroine, Candide and Cunégonde, are separated at the end of the first chapter and, like the traditional *héros de roman*, Candide must seek her throughout the world until he finds her – when he promptly loses her again and has to begin a second search. Every stage is marked by further disasters, until the lovers are finally reunited in Turkey. By this time Cunégonde has comprehensively lost her virginity, as well as her youthful looks and former sweet temper: yet Candide still finds an acceptable solution (see Text 7).

Why are these called 'contes philosophiques' and Voltaire a 'philosophe', the leader of the 'philosophes'? It is because he, and the other writers given this label, showed 'l'esprit philosophique', that is to say, the spirit of inquiry and the desire to pursue it in the face of claims by the Church or other institutions to superior authority. The philosophers Voltaire admired were scientists like Newton (he published *Eléments de la philosophie de Newton* in 1736), but even they were apt to stand on their authority and draw conclusions from inadequate data. *Micromégas* derives much comedy from the Earth scientists' certainty that they have all the right answers, a confidence that is unshaken even when they meet Micromégas, an inhabitant of Sirius 120,000 feet tall and his friend the Saturnian, a mere 6,000 feet. A deathless caricature of metaphysicians, and perhaps of the man learned in humanities in general, was provided in the person of Dr Pangloss (all-talk, from Greek *pan* and *glossa*), Candide's tutor, who affirms in the face of all disasters (exile, loss of an eye to syphilis, hanging etc.) that 'All is for the best in the best of all possible worlds'. An empty formula, since it simply means that nothing could be otherwise than it is, and therefore the world could not be any better – or worse.

TEXT 7 A HAPPY ENDING?

After all their adventures and misfortunes, all the principal characters in the story and several of the subsidiary ones have met up again, this time in Turkey. They have just been to the small-holding of an elderly Turk, who works it with his children and who offers them a delicious refreshment of his own produce. Candide, too, owns a little piece of land, which is at present uncultivated.

The repeated phrase 'il faut cultiver notre jardin' is often misquoted as 'il faut cultiver *son* jardin', one must cultivate one's [own] garden. As the last paragraph makes clear, this gospel of isolation is the very opposite of what Voltaire intended. The main meaning of 'cultiver' was (and still is) to cultivate in the agricultural sense: 'un cultivateur' is a farmer. The expression 'un homme cultivé' (an educated or cultured man) did not comme into use until the nineteenth century. Voltaire's is not a secret garden for 'cultivated' people.

Candide, en retournant dans sa métairie, fit de profondes réflexions sur le discours du Turc. Il dit à Pangloss et à Martin : 'Ce bon vieillard me paraît s'être fait un sort bien préférable à celui des six rois avec qui nous avons eu l'honneur de souper. – Les grandeurs, dit Pangloss, sont fort dangereuses, selon le rapport de tous les philosophes: car enfin Eglon, roi des Moabites, fut assassiné par Aod; Absalon fut pendu par les cheveux et percé de trois dards ; le roi Nadab, fils de Jéroboam, fut tué par Baasa ; le roi Ela par Zambri ; Ochosias, par Jéhu ; Athalia, par Joiada ; les rois Joachim, Jéchonias, Sédécias, furent esclaves. Vous savez comment périrent Crésus, Astyage, Darius, Denys de Syracuse, Pyrrhus, Persée, Annibal, Jugurtha, Arioviste, César, Pompée, Néron, Othon, Vitellius, Domitien, Richard II d'Angleterre, Edouard II, Henri VI, Richard III, Marie Stuart, Charles Ier, les trois Henri de France, l'empereur Henri IV ? Vous savez …

   Je sais aussi, dit Candide, qu'il faut cultiver notre jardin. – Vous avez raison, dit Pangloss : car, quand l'homme fut mis dans le jardin d'Eden, il y fut mis *ut operaretur eum*, pour qu'il y travaillât ; ce qui prouve que l'homme n'est pas né pour le repos. – Travaillons sans raisonner, dit Martin ; c'est le seul moyen de rendre la vie supportable.'

   Toute la petite société entra dans ce louable dessein ; chacun se mit à exercer ses talents.

   La petite terre rapporta beaucoup. Cunégonde était à la vérité bien laide, mais elle devint une excellente pâtissière ; Paquette broda ; la vieille eut soin du linge. Il n'y eut pas jusqu'à Frère Giroflée qui ne rendît service ; il fut un très bon menuisier, et même devint honnête homme ; et Pangloss disait quelquefois à Candide : 'Tous les événements sont enchaînés dans le meilleur des mondes possibles ; car si vous n'aviez pas été chassé d'un beau château à grands coups de pieds dans le derrière pour l'amour de mademoiselle Cunégonde ; si vous n'aviez pas été mis à l'Inquisition ; si vous n'aviez pas couru l'Amérique â pied, si vous n'aviez pas donné un bon coup d'épée au baron, si vous n'aviez pas perdu tous vos moutons du bon pays d'Eldorado, vous ne mangeriez pas ici des cédrats confits et des pistaches. – Cela est bien dit, dit Candide, mais il faut cultiver notre jardin'.

[Returning to his little farm, Candide thought deeply about what the Turk had said. He said to Pangloss and Martin, 'That old man seems to have made a much better life for himself than the six kings we had the honour of having supper with'.

'Greatness is very dangerous', said Pangloss, 'as all philosophers agree: for was not Eglon, the king of the Moabites, murdered by Aod; Absalom was hung by his hair and shot with three arrows; King Nadab, the son of Jeroboam, was killed by Baass; Ochosias, by Jehu; Athaliah by Joad; Kings Joachim, Jechoniah and Sedekiah were reduced to slavery. You know how Croesus died, and Astyages, Darius, Dionysius of Syracuse, Pyrrhus, Perseus, Hannibal, Jugurtha, Ariovistus, Caesar, Pompey, Nero, Otho, Vitellius, Domitian, Richard II of England, Edward II, Henry VI, Richard III, Mary Queen of Scots, Charles I, the three Henries of France, the emperor Henry IV. As you know …'

'I also know', said Candide, 'that we need to work on our garden'.

'Quite so', said Pangloss,'for when man was placed in the Garden of Eden he was put there *ut operaretur eum*, to work in it, which proves that man was not made for idleness. – Let's just work without so much talk, said Martin; that's the only way to make life tolerable'.

All the group agreed with this excellent plan, and each one began to put his or her talents to use.

> The little piece of land became highly productive. Cunégonde, it must be said, was very ugly now, but she became an excellent pastrycook; Paquette embroidered; the old lady took care of the linen. Even Brother Giroflée made himself useful. He proved to be an excellent carpenter and even became an honest man; and Pangloss used sometimes to say to Candide, 'Everything that happens is connected in the best of all possible worlds; for if you hadn't been kicked out of a beautiful chateau for the love of Mademoiselle Cunégonde, if you hadn't had to go before the Inquisition, if you hadn't walked all across South America, if you hadn't run through the baron with your sword, if you hadn't lost all the sheep you brought with you from Eldorado, you wouldn't be sitting here eating crystallised limes and pistachios.' 'True', said Candide, 'but we need to work on our garden'.]

Along with the medieval church, the Earth scientists in *Micromégas* affirm that the world and everything in it was made for man. Voltaire had always found that difficult to believe, and what finally made it impossible was the Lisbon earthquake of 1755, which with the ensuing tsunami and fire destroyed the city and killed some 50,000 people. Voltaire had written a long poem on this subject (*Poème sur le désastre de Lisbonne*, 1756), and one of the most memorable chapters of *Candide* is set in the city after the earthquake.

Apart from the *Lettres philosophiques* and *Candide,* a good introduction to Voltaire's ideas and style is the *Dictionnaire philosophique portatif* (1764). In one small volume, as its name implies, this is not a dictionary of the usual kind but a collection of short articles arranged in alphabetical order on such subjects as *Ange, Baptême, Christianisme, Dieu,* etc. The pieces are very varied in form, including brief essays, dialogues, little dramatic scenes and what could easily be described as further short 'contes philosophiques'. It was quickly banned and burnt in Geneva, Paris and Rome, managing to offend the orthodox everywhere.

Diderot

Denis Diderot (1713–84) was born in the provinces, at Langres, the son of a prosperous cutler. Despite being educated for the law he refused to follow any of the learned professions and led a hand-to-mouth existence for much of his life, living at first by literary hackwork – occasionally managing to publish essays of his own, but otherwise translating, editing the work of others and even writing a mildly pornographic novel, *Les bijoux indiscrets* (1748). His true life-work began in 1750 when he accepted the commission to edit the *Encyclopédie*. The publishers had had in mind simply a translation of Ephraim Chambers' *Cyclopaedia* (1728), but under Diderot's direction the project developed into something far more ambitious, with the eventual title *Encyclopédie, ou Dictionnaire raisonné des sciences, des arts et des métiers.* It was Diderot's task to find the contributors and commission the articles, and at first he was able to line up some of the best-known names in the intellectual world of the time, including Montesquieu, Voltaire, Rousseau and the mathematician and physicist d'Alembert, who was to be his co-editor until 1758. At that time Diderot was left solely responsible for the vast undertaking, plagued by censorship and intermittent bans on publication. As the hostility of the authorities became apparent, some contributors deserted, and Diderot had to write more and more of the articles himself. It was not until 1772 that the last of the planned volumes appeared: seventeen volumes of text and eleven of admirably detailed plates, many of them illustrating the craft and industrial processes of the various trades, the 'métiers' of the title. It was an entirely novel idea that ladies and gentlemen should wish to know about such things.

As well as articles for the *Encyclopédie,* Diderot was writing plays and dramatic theory, novels (*La Religieuse* (The Nun), *Jacques le fataliste)* and philosophical dialogues like *Le Rêve de d'Alembert* (D'Alembert's Dream), *Supplément au voyage de Bougainville* and *Le Neveu de Rameau*. In the *Supplément,* two characters, A and B, exchange reflections on Bougainville's recent journey to Tahiti and the customs he discovered there, while *Le Neveu de Rameau* is a dialogue between Moi – supposedly Diderot himself – and Lui, a nephew of the composer Rameau, whose amoral approach to life appears to scandalize 'Moi'. (But we remember the faux-naïf letter-writers of Pascal and Voltaire and take his shocked reactions with a pinch of salt.) Of all these brilliant productions, however, as original in ideas as form, none was published in his lifetime – *Le neveu de Rameau* not until 1823. Many of his most original works were circulated in manuscript, thanks to a remark-able institution called the *Correspondance littéraire.* Created in 1747 by one Raynal, but run from 1753 onwards by the German man of letters Friedrich Melchior Grimm, it employed copyists to reproduce works likely to fall foul of the censors, which were then circulated to a select and secret list of subscribers, most of them outside France. The list included, as well as many German princelings, the king of Poland, the sister of Frederick II of Prussia, and no less a person than the Empress Catherine II of Russia, who was to become Diderot's patron. From 1759 onwards Diderot took over partial responsibility for the *Correspondance littéraire,* while still working on the *Encyclopédie.* In 1762 when he felt obliged to sell his library to provide for his daughter, the Empress Catherine bought it *en viager* (that is to say, Diderot would continue to use it until his death). Not only this, she paid him a yearly salary to act as her librarian, though the books themselves remained in Paris. This generous act finally gave Diderot some financial security.

The topics addressed by Diderot bring him closer to what modern Anglo-Saxon philosophers would recognize as their dis-cipline than do the far-ranging interests of Voltaire. He wrote two essays on sense-perception and its relation to reason and morals: *Lettre sur les aveugles* (Letter on blind people, 1749), which earned him three months imprisonment in the castle at Vincennes, and *Lettre sur les sourds et muets,* (Letter on the deaf and dumb, 1751).

In his writings about human feelings and behaviour he showed himself a materialist – that is, he rejected the idea, held from Plato to Descartes, that human beings were a cohabitation of matter (the body) and spirit (the soul). Instead he argued that matter, through a process of development, could begin to feel and eventually to think. In this sense he anticipated the idea of evolution, and some undeveloped passages in his writings also hint at the idea of natural selection. In any case, he expected advances in philosophy to come from the development of the natural sciences, of which he had a better understanding than either Voltaire or Rousseau.

Rousseau

Of the 'philosophes' **Jean-Jacques Rousseau** (1712–78) is the one most likely to figure in a modern history of philosophy course. He owes this place to his treatise *Du Contrat social* (1762), which is usually placed, after Hobbes's *Leviathan*, at the beginning of modern political philosophy. The 'social contract' in question is the one that, according to Rousseau, marks the origin of all settled states. Governments owe their legitimacy not to, say, God's ordinance, but to the consent of the citizens. When and how the governed gave this consent, and why they can be thought still to be giving it, are what Rousseau tries to explain in the book. He also suggests political arrangements that will make the form of government the best expression of what he calls the 'general will'. These were very powerful if very abstract ideas (Rousseau had no practical experience of politics or government whatever), and are thought to have influenced both the American and the French Revolutions.

Rousseau's influence was felt not only in the world of politics, however: he is said to have inspired a whole new set of feelings about love, child-rearing and nature, and so to have helped originate the European movement called Romanticism. How could one man do all this? And especially such a man as Rousseau was.

Rousseau was born at Geneva, the son of a watchmaker. His mother died when he was ten and he was left to his own devices early in life, soon forming the habit of relying on patrons. His first important patron, from the age of fifteen, was a much older lady called Madame de Warens. After a few years his relationship with her became sexual, but he continued calling her 'Maman' and living largely at her expense until his late twenties. About the age of thirty he moved to Paris, hoping to make his fortune from a new system of musical notation he had devised, but nothing came of this and he accepted a secretaryship to a nobleman with whom he soon quarrelled. In 1744, while living a hand-to-mouth existence of music-copying and literary hackwork, he formed what was to be a long-lasting relationship with Thérèse Levasseur, an illiterate seamstress who became his housekeeper. He never taught her to read, and kept her as far as possible apart from his educated friends, but he did give her five children, all of whom he persuaded her to abandon to the foundling-hospital. When this fact became generally known, and horrified even his usually pretty unsentimental literary friends, he argued that he had done it so that in later life his children would not have to face society's cruelty to bastards. (The obvious solution to this problem does not seem to have suggested itself to him, and it is unlikely in any case that the children would have lived to grow up, given mortality rates at the *Enfants-trouvés*). He does not seem to have felt that the choices he made as a parent in any way disqualified him from writing a book on how to bring up children, and *Emile, ou l'Education* (1762), a treatment in semi-fictional form of the model upbringing offered to a fortunate boy, was a great success and enjoyed two centuries of influence in educationist circles (see Text 8). It is surprising but true that Rousseau writes very perceptively about the psychology of children; he must either have managed to observe them closely at some stage in his unsettled life, or have had excellent recall of his own thought processes as a child.

The years 1761 and 1762 were his period of greatest success: in 1761 he published the long letter-novel *Julie, ou la Nouvelle Héloïse*, now quite unreadable but much read and loved well into to the nineteenth century, and in 1762 *Du Contrat social* and *Emile*.

From 1765 to 1770 he lived in England, where he quarrelled with everyone who tried to help him, notably the philosopher Hume. Towards the end of his life he sank into something resembling paranoia, though he was still constantly helped by faithful patrons.

In his last years his writings became mostly autobiographical, from the *Confessions,* written in 1765–70 but not published until 1782, after his death, to the *Dialogues de Rousseau juge de Jean-Jacques,* written between 1772 and 1776 and published in 1782, and the *Rêveries du promeneur solitaire* (Reveries of the solitary walker), written between 1776 and 1779 and published in 1782, which remained very popular throughout the nineteenth century.

How to account for Rousseau's popularity throughout the Romantic period? One possible explanation might be that, in contrast to Christian teaching about original sin, he taught that man was originally good. These origins are very remote – lost in the mists of time – and life in organized society has made men bad, a process that he did not believe could be reversed. The account that he gives of the state of nature in the *Discours sur l'origine de l'inégalité* owes nothing to observation nor indeed, one might say, to common sense. But he is aware of that: in his Preface he notoriously says, 'Commençons donc par écarter tous les faits, car ils ne touchent point à la question' (Let us then begin by setting all the facts on one side, as they have nothing to do with the matter). From first principles he derives a picture of early Man (who is definitely a man) as a hunter-gatherer, wandering alone in the forest. Reproduction must somehow have taken place, but there is no family life and men do not recognize their own children. As soon as any form of collective life (families, clans, settled agriculture, property) takes shape, evil enters the world. But the belief in essential goodness persists, whether applied to man in general or to himself. 'I am good – if bad things happen around me, society is to blame': it is unjust to father this doctrine in its crudest form on Rousseau, but we can see its origin in his writings.

TEXT 8 EDUCATION, A SAD NECESSITY

These are the opening lines of Book I of Rousseau's *Emile*. The asterisk after 'tendre et prévoyante mère' introduces a page-long footnote on mothers, how the law should give them more authority over their offspring, and how their 'tendresse' is so much better for young children than the 'insensibilité' of fathers. All these ideas were to be very influential in the ensuing decades.

Tout est bien, sortant de la main de l'auteur des choses : tout dégénère entre les mains de l'homme. Il force une terre à nourrir les productions d'une autre ; un arbre à produire les fruits d'un autre. Il mêle et confond les climats, les éléments, les saisons. Il mutile son chien, son cheval, son esclave. Il bouleverse tout, il défigure tout : il aime la difformité, les monstres. Il ne veut rien tel que l'a fait la nature, pas même l'homme; il le faut dresser pour lui comme un cheval de manège ; il le faut contourner à sa mode comme un arbre de son jardin.

Sans cela tout iroit plus mal encore, et nôtre espèce ne veut pas être façonnée à demi. Dans l'état où sont désormais les choses, un homme abandonné dès sa naissance à lui-même seroit le plus défiguré de tous. Les préjugés, l'autorité, la nécessité, l'exemple, toutes les institutions sociales dans lesquelles nous nous trouvons submergés, étoufferoient en lui la nature, et ne mettroient rien à la place. Elle y seroit comme un arbrisseau que le hazard fait naître au milieu d'un chemin, et que les passants font bientôt périr en le heurtant de toutes parts et le pliant dans tous les sens.

C'est à toi que je m'adresse, tendre et prévoyante mère*, qui sus t'écarter de la grande route, et garantir l'arbrisseau naissant du choc des opinions humaines. Cultive, arrose la jeune plante avant qu'elle meure; ses fruits feront un jour tes délices. Forme de bonne heure une enceinte autour de l'âme de ton enfant : un autre en peut marquer le circuit : mais toi seule y dois poser la barrière.

[Everything is good as it comes from the hand of the maker of all things: everything degenerates in the hands of man. He forces one land to grow the crops of another, one tree to produce the fruits of another.

He mixes and confuses climates, elements, seasons. He mutilates his dog, his horse, his slave.

He turns everthing upside down, disfigures everything. He loves deformed things, monsters. Nothing will do for him as nature made it, even man; a child must be trained up for him like a dressage horse, fashioned like the trees of his garden.

Without such training the child would fare even worse: our species cannot be trained by halves. As things now stand, a man left to himself from birth would be the most disfigured of all. Prejudices, authority, necessity, example: all the social institutions by which we find ourselves submerged would stifle nature in him, and put nothing in its place. It [nature in him] would be like a tree-shoot springing up by chance in the middle of a path, which the passers-by soon kill by treading on it from all sides and bending it in all directions.

This book is addressed to you, tender and far-sighted mother, who have already chosen to turn aside from the trodden path, and protect the new-born sapling from the impact of human opinions. Cultivate, water the young plant lest it die; its fruits will one day be your delight. Form without delay a protective barrier around your child's soul; another may trace out its circuit, but it is you alone must build it.]

The novel

Popular literary forms in the eighteenth century were the memoir- and letter-novel. Both of these allow the author to pretend that the story he tells actually happened. A frame-story or preface usually recounts the finding of the manuscript, of which the author pretends to be merely the editor. This allows him to distance himself from any reprehensible behaviour by the characters. The readership for any eighteenth-century novel would have been very small compared to those reached in the nineteenth century. It was assumed that readers, like the characters in most of the stories, would be ladies and gentlemen, since only they would have had the money to buy novels or the leisure to read them. There was therefore much less need for description and explanation of setting and manners than in the later works. Since the principal subject of novels was love, it was thought that most novel-readers were likely to be women, and many ladies wrote successfully for this market. The novels still read today, however, are mostly by men. Two of the most rewarding are *Manon Lescaut* by the **Abbé Prévost** (1697–1763), and *Les Liaisons dangereuses* by **Pierre Choderlos de Laclos** (1741–1803).

Manon Lescaut originally appeared as Volume VII of a ten-volume memoir-novel called *Mémoires d'un homme de qualité* (Memoirs of a Gentleman, 1731). The story, supposedly told to the 'homme de qualité' by its hero or victim, the Chevalier des Grieux, is of his demoralising love for an unworthy woman (girl, rather, since she is sixteen at the beginning of the action and dies only a couple of years later). Des Grieux is a Rousseau-style hero before his time, a good person who somehow keeps doing bad things, whereas Manon is cheerfully immoral throughout. The story succeeded with readers from its first appearance, and was soon (1733) issued as a single volume. It has never been out of print since, has been filmed eight times and made the subject of two ballets and four operas (by Auber, Massenet, Puccini and Hans-Werner Henze).

Figure 3 Laclos, *Les Liaisons dangereuses*, London, 1796, illustration to Letter XLVIII

Les Liaisons dangereuses is a brilliantly complex letter-novel. Most such works have two, or at the most three or four, correspondents, but Laclos manages to keep seven principals in play, along with various servants, confessors and the like, to unfold a complicated but gripping story of love, lust, deception, vanity and self-reproach. No subsequent letter-novel approaches its quality, and indeed the genre lost its predominant place as the nineteenth century approached. Despite the inherent difficulty of filming a book not only written in letters, but in which the key events are the writing and reception of letters, Roger Vadim attempted an updated version in 1959, with good success, under the title *Les Liaisons dangereuses 1960*. The book seems to have aroused particular interest in England and America in the mid-1980s, when there were four dramatic adaptations, two for the stage, by Howard Davies and Christopher Hampton, and two films, by Stephen Frears *(Dangerous Liaisons)* and Milos Forman *(Valmont)*. In 1999 a further updating *(Cruel Intentions)* reset the story in an American high school.

TEXT 9 A CLEVER GIRL EDUCATES HERSELF

Married at fifteen to a much older man, Madame de Merteuil, the heroine-villainess of *Les Liaisons dangereuses,* once she has lost her virginity, pursues her 'observations' with male servants and country neighbours much below her rank. (This is safer, as they do not know the 'people who matter', and so cannot damage her reputation by gossip). 'Moralistes' in the second paragraph must here mean 'teachers of morals'. (*Les Liaisons danguruses*, letter LXXXI)

La maladie de M. de Merteuil vint interrompre de si douces occupations ; il fallait le suivre à la ville, où il venait chercher des secours. Il mourut, comme vous savez, peu de temps

après ; et quoique, à tout prendre, je n'eusse pas à me plain-
dre de lui, je n'en sentis pas moins vivement le prix de la
liberté qu'allait me donner mon veuvage, et je me promis
bien d'en profiter.

Ma mère comptait que j'entrerais au couvent, ou revi-
endrais vivre avec elle. Je refusai l'un et l'autre parti ; et tout
ce que j'accordai à la décence, fut de retourner dans cette
même campagne, où il me restait bien encore quelques
observations à faire.

Je les fortifiai par le secours de la lecture ; mais ne croyez
pas qu'elle fût toute du genre que vous la supposez. J'étudiai
nos mœurs dans les romans ; nos opinions dans les philosophes ; je cherchai même dans nos plus sévères moralistes
ce qu'ils exigeaient de nous, et je m'assurai ainsi de ce qu'on
pouvait faire, de ce qu'on devait penser, et de ce qu'il fallait
paraître. Une fois fixée sur ces trois objets, le dernier seul
présenta quelques difficultés dans son exécution ; j'espérai
les vaincre et j'en méditai les moyens.

[M. de Merteuil's illness supervening, interrupted these charming
pursuits; I had to follow him to the city, where he went to seek
help. He died, as you know, shortly afterwards, and though, all in
all, I had no reason to complain of him as a husband, I still had a
lively sense of the new freedom I should enjoy as a widow, and
resolved to make the most of it.

My mother thought that I would enter a convent, or go back to
live with her. I refused both alternatives, and my only concession to
propriety was to return to the same country estate, where I still had
some further observations to make.

I supplemented them with reading, but do not suppose that it
was all reading of the kind you imagine. I studied people's behaviour in novels, their opinions in the philosophers, and I even went
to our severest moralists to see what they required of us, and so
gained a certain knowledge of what one could do, what one ought
to think, and what one must seem to be. Once clear on those three
points, I saw some difficulties only in the third; I hoped to overcome these and set my mind on the means of doing so.]

The last great memoir-novel in the eighteenth-century style was in fact written in the early nineteenth century: *Adolphe* by Benjamin Constant (1767–1830) was written in 1807 but not published until 1816, when the author was 49. Constant was a political philosopher and active politician: this short book, initially published in London anonymously, was his only published fictional work. Despite beginning with the usual found-manuscript story, it is plainly autobiographical. Its apparent echoes of Constant's long relationship with Mme de Stael, the most famous or notorious literary lady of the day, ensured it a *succès de scandale*. But its timeless subject (how to end a failing relationship), psychological penetration and lucid style have given it a continuing place in the canon.

One eighteenth-century novelist that many literary people would have heard of but few before the 1960s would have read (Flaubert was one) was **Donatien-Alphonse-François, marquis de Sade** (1740–1814), since his writings could be published only clandestinely, for sale to specialized markets. His horrible novels usually quickly provoke disgust and boredom, but the twentieth-century Surrealists praised them for their shock value, and later literary figures supported their publication, either in the name of complete freedom of speech or because, in their sheer crushing repetitiveness, they somehow transcended 'literary' values. Some critics still accept Sade's own valuation of himself as a philosopher. But his dogmatic materialism and belief in 'Nature, red in tooth and claw' hardly deserve that title. The way in which the spokespersons for these ideas invariably win all the arguments, as a prelude to gleefully enforcing their will upon the unfortunate believers in affection, morality or religion, has little that is philosophical about it.

The theatre

Tragedy was still officially the most highly respected form in the eighteenth century, but, perhaps because of the continuing influence of Corneille and Racine, most tragedies of this period, even Voltaire's, are derivative and uninspired, and are never revived today. The great eighteenth-century dramatists are writers of comedy: **Pierre Carlet de Chamblain Marivaux** (1688–1763) and **Pierre-Augustin Caron de Beaumarchais** (1732–99). Marivaux's plays, many of them written for performance by the Italiens, the theatre company descended from the *commedia dell'arte* players who had first settled in Paris in Louis XIV's time, almost always have love as their subject, with plots based on misunderstanding, disguise, mismatches and pique, but always leading to a happy ending. The delicate language in which the actors work their way through these various puzzles is known in French as *marivaudage*.

Marivaux was also a novelist, the author of *Le Paysan parvenu* (The Peasant Boy's Success, 1735–6) and *La Vie de Marianne* (1731–41), both tales told by young people of low or doubtful birth, recounting their struggles and progress in the world.

Beaumarchais' two great comedies, *Le Barbier de Séville* (1775) and *Le Mariage de Figaro* (1784) are probably even better known as the source of the operas by Rossini and Mozart, but they are well worth reading, or better still seeing, for their spirit and humour and management of complicated plots.

A new kind of play that had some success in the later eighteenth century was the so-called *drame bourgeois*, a serious play in prose. It showed contemporary, middle-class characters facing moral dilemmas and taking noble decisions, thus lending to such characters some of the dignity that tragedy had reserved to kings and heroes. Beaumarchais wrote some plays in this vein also, notably *La Mère coupable* (1792) the third in the Figaro trilogy. Diderot had both contributed to the genre with *Le Fils naturel* (1757, not produced until 1771) and *Le Père de famille* (1758, produced 1761), and written its theory. Alas, these plays now seem stagy in the worst sense, hardly less artificial than the tragedy they aimed to replace.

5

The nineteenth century I (1800–52): Realists and Romantics

Many historians would like the nineteenth century, the century of revolutions, to run from 1789 to 1917, from the French Revolution to the Russian. Certainly 1789 to 1852 in France was a period of successive dramatic political changes.

The Revolution of 1789, at first a bourgeois revolution, which established a constitutional monarchy, was succeeded by a Republic (1792), then the Terror (1793), the Convention (1794), the Directoire (1794–99), then the Consulat (1799) with Napoleon as First Consul. Not content with this role, he proclaimed himself Emperor in 1804. After his final defeat at Waterloo in 1815, royal power was restored in the person of the two elderly brothers of Louis XVI: Louis XVIII (d. 1824) and his successor Charles X (Louis XVII having died as a child in captivity). Charles X was deposed by another revolution in July 1830, and replaced by a more amenable king from the lesser, Orléans branch of the royal family, Louis-Philippe, the so-called Citizen King, who reigned as a constitutional monarch until he too was deposed in 1848. His reign is called the July Monarchy.

The revolution of 1848 at first established a republic, called the Second Republic in memory of 1792. But Louis-Napoléon

Bonaparte, the nephew of the original Napoleon, stood for and was elected to the Assembly, and then to the Presidency of the Republic, and three years later had himself proclaimed Emperor as Napoleon III (Napoleon I's son, styled Napoleon II by his supporters, having died in exile in 1832). The Second Empire lasted from 1852 until France's crushing defeat by the Prussians in 1870, when it was replaced by the Third Republic, which lasted until the defeat of 1940.

This chequered history means that a writer who was born in the late eighteenth century like Stendhal (b. 1783: his real name was Henri Beyle) or Honoré de Balzac (b. 1799) could remember the glory and fall of Napoleon as well as the reactionary atmosphere of the Restoration, the Revolution of 1830 and the more easy-going, get-rich-quick life of the July Monarchy. Stendhal died in 1842, Balzac in 1850 (exhausted, it was said, by the work of writing his ninety-two novels, his journalism and his endless financial crises). But Victor Hugo (1802–85) as an old man could remember, as well as the First Empire and the Restoration, the Revolutions of 1830 and 1848, in the latter of which he took an active part, the coup d'état of 1852, the end of the Second Empire in 1870 and the founding of the Third Republic, of which he became a figurehead and hero.

It is not surprising that the writing of men who lived through such times should closely reflect the society that they lived in, and the great novels of this period are the in the mode called 'realist' (though neither Stendhal nor Balzac ever used this word).

The 'realist' novel typically has a nearly contemporary subject, or one taken from very recent history. Stendhal's *Le Rouge et le noir*, published in 1830, is set at the very end of the Restoration, just before the July Revolution, while Balzac's *La Peau de chagrin*, published in 1831, is set just after it and makes many references to the events of the preceding year; the young intellectuals and artists that make up its cast are already disillusioned with the new democratic ideal (see Text 11). His *Le Père Goriot* (1834, set in 1820) and *Illusions perdues* (1837–43, set in 1821–2) are similarly rooted in recent events and offer detailed descriptions of contemporary settings and social mores.

The 1830s and 1840s also saw the beginnings of industrialization in France (much later than in England). Of particular interest from our point of view were advances in printing methods and particularly in paper-making, which allowed copy to be reproduced much more cheaply and permitted the development of a periodical press (newspapers and magazines). Novels were often published in parts, at first in the fortnightly or monthly literary magazines but eventually as supplements (*feuilletons*) to daily newspapers. Other successful kinds of ephemeral publication included guides to fashionable life and manners, 'anatomies' ('*physiologies*') of different social types, pamphlets of literary and dramatic criticism, handbooks to art exhibitions and travel guides. All the best-remembered writers of the period worked in these forms: most notably Balzac, but also Stendhal and **Théophile Gautier** (1811–72), who was not only a poet, novelist and author of gothic tales, but for forty years a journalist, writing music, art and theatre criticism, and a composer of libretti for operas and scenarios for ballets. Charles Baudelaire (1821–66) was also a journalist by his twenties, publishing guides to the Salons (the annual art exhibitions) of 1845 and 1846.

Balzac

The family of **Honoré de Balzac** (1799–1850) had intended him for the law, and as a very young man he did work as a lawyer's clerk. But at twenty he announced his career was to be in literature, and he struggled through extreme poverty at first, always believing that fame and fortune would one day be his. He published sensational novels under pseudonyms, anonymous journalism and humorous short books with mock-learned titles commenting on contemporary manners and fashions: *Physiologie du mariage: ou Méditations de philosophie éclectique sur le bonheur et le malheur conjugal* (Anatomy of Marriage, or Eclectic Philosophical Meditations on Marital Fortune and Misfortune, 1829); *Traîté de la vie élégante* (Treatise on Fashionable Life, 1830). His first real break-through, *Les Chouans* (The Rebels, 1829), a story of the Revolution, began a twenty-year period of astonishing productivity during which he wrote more than ninety novels and long-short stories. Among the best-known are *La Peau de chagrin* (The Wild Ass's Skin, 1831), *Le Père Goriot* (Old Goriot, first published in parts in the *Revue de Paris* in 1834–35), *Illusions perdues* (Lost Illusions), which appeared in three parts in 1837–42, and *Splendeurs et misères des courtisanes* (Highs and Lows in the Lives of Courtesans), a group of four related tales published between 1838 and 1847.

In all of these novels the hero is a very young man who battles against social barriers to realise his personal ambitions. So far, so autobiographical. But whereas Balzac's own family was only one generation away from the peasantry (his father, François Balssa, had made his fortune supplying the revolutionary armies, like old Goriot in the novel of that name), his heroes Raphael de Valentin in *La Peau de chagrin*, Eugène de Rastignac in *Le Père Goriot* and Lucien de Rubempré in *Illusions perdues* and *Splendeurs et misères* all have the magic 'de' in their names which shows they spring from pre-Revolutionary aristocratic families (Balzac's 'de' was his own invention). All, however, have been reduced to poverty if not penury by the beginning of the action. Both Eugène and Lucien are inhabited by a fierce desire to succeed in the new, bourgeois-dominated world, and to restore their family's rightful fortunes (both have mothers and sisters in genteel poverty whom they intend, in the long run, to support). Devising such heroes allowed Balzac to appeal to the widest possible readership: not only the leisured classes and their womenfolk (though novel-reading was often regarded as chiefly a feminine pursuit), but even young bourgeois, clerks and students who could sympathize with the heroes' desperate shifts, or their older and more successful counterparts who could look back on their penniless youth with amusement. At the same time, the heroes' striving for money and position, which might have appeared sordid to some readers of the 1830s, could be redeemed by the thought that they were trying only to reclaim what was rightfully theirs. (Stendhal had gone much further in *Le Rouge et le noir* by choosing in Julien Sorel a genuinely lower-class hero, little more than a peasant. Julien's naked ambition, and sexual relationships with upper-class women, gave offence to many, and the book was a commercial failure.)

A man of tremendous energy, both physical and intellectual, Balzac typically had several writing projects on the go at once, as well as various money-making schemes, and, though he was not at all handsome, love affairs, usually with aristocratic ladies. Always pursued by deadlines and creditors, he would work all night, fuelled by black coffee. None of this made for an elegant style, and he drove his printers to despair by virtually rewriting whole pages at the proof stage. Nevertheless the energy of his writing, and his sheer productiveness, meant that though his purely commercial schemes all failed (from printing and type-founding to magazine publishing to trying to grow pineapples on the outskirts of Paris), he eventually made several fortunes by his writing, and lost them again by extravagant house-buying and collecting.

What characterizes his novels is, first, a mass of detail about social habits, settings, clothes, food, the objects that surround his characters and that, he believed, allowed the socially expert viewer to 'read' them, assign them to the right milieu and, up to a point, predict their actions. Like many European readers of his day, he was a great admirer of Walter Scott, and felt that Scott's detailed accounts of medieval architecture, costume, armour, weapons and so forth made his historical stories believable.

He decided to do something similar for the present and the recent past. The level of visual detail in, say, the description of Mme Vauquer's boarding-house at the beginning of *Le Père Goriot*, is almost hallucinatory, but can seem excessive to readers who have grown up with the cinema and television, and expect all that to be dealt with by a few establishing shots. However there is no doubt that his detailed descriptions appealed to readers of his day, perhaps because his was a society of growing social mobility, both upwards and downwards, in which readers had become genuinely curious about how people from different social classes lived, dressed, ate and conducted their love lives. We shall meet one such socially mobile person in the next chapter.

Balzac had two further completely original ideas for novel-writing: one, what the French call 'le retour des personnages', the use of recurring characters, and the other, his attempt to bind all his fiction together in one huge, structured whole, which he decided to call *La Comédie humaine.*

He conceived the idea of recurring characters while writing *Le Père Goriot*. His naive young hero from the south-west was originally to have been called Eugène de Massiac. But Balzac had already given the hero of *La Peau de chagrin* a foil in the person of Eugène de Rastignac, a clever, humorous southerner, a refugee from aristocratic poverty living by his wits somewhere between the worlds of journalism and high society in 1831. In the course of writing, Massiac became Rastignac, so that we now saw the same character ten years younger and only at the beginning of his battle to succeed. Rastignac would eventually appear in at least a further seven novels, not all in chronological order, and end up as a successful politician and a peer. From *Le Père Goriot* onwards, Balzac created a cast of eventually some three thousand named characters, at least six hundred of whom appear and reappear in different social settings at different stages in their lives. Some rise in the world like Rastignac, others fall like Baron Hulot in *La Cousine Bette,* while the most regular reappearances are made by the middle-class professional characters like Bianchon the doctor (a medical student in *Le Père Goriot* and hospital consultant by *La Cousine Bette*: Balzac is said to have asked for him on his deathbed) or Derville the lawyer. It is this complex network of vivid characters that leads critics to talk of Balzac as having created a parallel world. He himself said that he wanted to 'faire concurrence à l'Etat Civil' (rival the registry [of births, marriages and deaths]).

He says this in his preface to the *Comédie Humaine*, the huge collection of his novels and tales, which was to have been the work of his final years. This was both an enormous artistic and intellectual undertaking and, as one would expect of Balzac, an ambitious financial scheme, since it allowed him to reissue all his earlier writings with a new syndicate of publishers and profit from them again. The first collected edition, which began to appear in 1842, arranged the existing novels and tales into a three-part scheme with the serious-sounding titles *Etudes de mœurs* (Studies of social behaviour), *Etudes philosophiques* and *Etudes analytiques*. Considerable rewriting of individual stories was done: in particular, names of many minor characters were changed in order to identify them with already existing figures in other books, and thus to tighten the network of recurring characters. In 1845, Balzac produced a catalogue for a new edition, which would have involved more rearrangement to produce a truly scientifically satisfying plan. Like the periodic table, the new structure contained gaps, which Balzac maintained he intended to fill with new novels. He wrote a further four before his death in 1850, leaving two unfinished and several of his gaps unfilled.

Stendhal

Henri Beyle (1783–1842), who published all his works under the name of **Stendhal**, was sixteen years older than Balzac, but did not become known as a novelist until middle age. An officer in Napoleon's army at seventeen, his posting to Milan began a love affair with Italy that was to last all his life. After resigning his commission in 1802 and living in Paris for a few years, he returned to the army in 1806 and served in the supply arm in Germany, Russia and Austria. Resigning again in 1813 aged thirty, he was able to return to his beloved Milan and live there for a further seven years. He appears to have had no ambition at this time to write fiction, and whereas at twenty Balzac was learning his trade by writing highly coloured tales of adventure under various assumed names, Stendhal at thirty had published only short, rather dilettantish works of criticism containing much borrowed material: lives of composers, a history of Italian painting and accounts of Rome, Naples and Florence in 1817. Returning to Paris in 1821, he continued at first to publish in this vein: another composer (Rossini), more 'Promenades dans Rome', an attempt to define and argue for modernity in literature (*Racine et Shakespeare)*. But towards the end of the decade he produced his first novels, each of them at attempt at utter topicality: *Armance* (1827), with its subtitle 'Quelques scènes d'un salon de Paris en 1827', and *Le Rouge et le noir* (1830), with its subtitle 'Chronique de 1830'. *Armance* attracted little notice and *Le Rouge et le noir* not much more, and much of that negative. The tale of Julien Sorel, a sensitive but fiercely ambitious small-town boy who makes his way first as tutor to a family of the local gentry, where he seduces the wife, and then by entering a seminary, which he leaves to be secretary in the Parisian house of a great noble where the daughter seduces him (see Text 10): a story like this, ending in attempted murder and the hero's death on the scaffold, offended many of its original readers, as did the author's evident nostalgia for the Napoleonic period and contempt for the Restoration political regime.

The style of *Le Rouge et le noir* was also unlike what readers expected. The hero is in no way idealized, though the reader's sympathy is certainly invited for him, to a large extent by the use of humour. The lengthy descriptions so important to Balzac are here absent: Stendhal, once he started writing, worked extremely fast and had not the patience to describe costumes, room settings and so forth, though his publisher complained that readers missed these details. Instead, Stendhal gives us his characters' thoughts, what are sometimes called their inner monologues – Julien's all the time, but other sympathetic characters quite frequently, and often more than one character's thoughts in the same scene.

TEXT 10 A FIRST NIGHT TOGETHER

Mathilde de La Mole, the daughter of a nobleman, a proud and haughty girl, has sent a note inviting Julien Sorel, her father's secretary, to come to her room by night using a ladder. He fears a trap but feels he must go. He has had one love affair before: this will be her first.

Elle avait décidé que s'il osait arriver chez elle, avec le secours de l'échelle du jardinier, ainsi qu'il lui était prescrit, elle serait toute à lui. Mais jamais l'on ne dit d'un ton plus froid et plus poli des choses aussi tendres. Jusque-là ce rendez-vous était glacé. C'était à faire prendre l'amour en haine. Quelle leçon de morale pour une jeune imprudente ! Vaut-il la peine de perdre son avenir pour un tel moment ?

Après de longues incertitudes, qui eussent pu paraître à un observateur superficiel l'effet de la haine la plus décidée, tant les sentiments qu'une femme se doit à elle-même avaient de peine à céder même à une volonté aussi ferme, Mathilde finit par être pour lui une maitresse aimable.

A la vérité, ces transports étaient un peu *voulus*. L'amour passionné était encore plutôt un modèle à imiter qu'une réalité.

Mademoiselle de La Mole croyait remplir un devoir envers elle-même et envers son amant. Le pauvre garçon, se disait-elle, a été d'une bravoure achevée, il doit être heureux, ou bien c'est moi qui manque de caractère. Mais elle aurait voulu racheter au prix d'une éternité de malheur la nécessité cruelle ou elle se trouvait.

Malgré la violence affreuse qu'elle se faisait, elle fut parfaitement maitresse de ses paroles.

Aucun regret, aucun reproche ne vinrent gâter cette nuit qui sembla singulière plutôt qu'heureuse à Julien. Quelle différence, grand Dieu ! avec son dernier séjour de vingt-quatre heures à Verrières ! Ces belles façons de Paris ont trouvé le secret de tout gâter, meme l'amour, se disait-il avec une injustice extrême.

Il se livrait à ces réflexions debout dans une des grandes armoires d'acajou où on l'avait fait entrer aux premiers bruits entendus dans l'appartement voisin, qui était celui de Madame de La Mole. Mathilde suivit sa mère à la messe, les femmes quittèrent bientôt l'appartement, et Julien s'échappa facilement avant qu'elles ne revinssent terminer leurs travaux.

Il monta à cheval et chercha les endroits les plus solitaires d'une des forêts voisines de Paris. Il était bien plus étonné qu'heureux.

[She had decided that if he dared to come to her room using the gardener's ladder, as he had been instructed, she would give herself to him. But her words of love were spoken in the coldest and most polite tone imaginable. So far the meeting had been chilly in the extreme. It would have turned one against the very idea of love. What a moral lesson for an imprudent girl! Is a moment like this worth the sacrifice of her future?

After much hesitation, in which a superficial observer might have seen the effect of the most definite hatred, so fiercely did a woman's self-respect struggle against the strength of her determination, Mathilde eventually behaved to him like a loving mistress.

In truth, her transports were somewhat *deliberate*. Passionate love was still a model to be imitated rather than something real.

Mademoiselle de la Mole felt that she was fulfilling a duty both to herself and to her lover. The poor boy has been so brave, she thought, he must have his reward or I shall have let myself down. But she would have given an eternity of torment to escape the cruel situation in which she now found herself trapped.

In spite of the dreadful violence she was doing to herself, she remained in complete control of her speech.

No regrets, no reproaches came to spoil the night, which seemed remarkable rather than delightful to Julien. Good Lord, how unlike his last twenty-four hours at Verrières! That's Paris people for you, he said to himself (most unfairly): their fine manners manage to spoil everything, even love.

He was thinking these things standing up in one of the great mahogany wardrobes, where he had been hidden at the first sounds from the next room, which was Madame de la Mole's. Mathilde went with her mother to Mass, the maids soon left the room and Julien easily escaped before they came back to finish their work.

He jumped on horseback and made for the loneliest stretches of one of the forests near Paris. He felt much more astonishment than happiness.]

The language used is plain: Stendhal never tries to work up emotional effects as other novelists of the time expected to do. Julien's death is a striking example of this. We are told that he was concerned to die bravely and feared that he might not, but when he walked out into the fresh morning air, 'Marcher au grand air fut pour lui une sensation délicieuse … Allons, tout va bien, se dit-il, je ne manque point de courage'. He remembers (for one sentence) brief moments of happiness: then the actual execution is described thus: 'Tout se passa simplement, convenablement, et de sa part sans aucune affectation' (Everything passed off simply, appropriately and with no affectation on his part). No Sydney Carton speeches from the scaffold, no authorial soaring music at the end. No wonder readers of 1830 felt cheated.

Stendhal published no further novels until 1839, though it appears he was working on a story of contemporary French life, *Lucien Leuwen*, which was left incomplete at his death in 1842. Instead of finishing it, he completed and published, in 1839, *La Chartreuse de Parme* (The Charterhouse of Parma), which is set in the small Duchy of Parma between 1815 and 1830. (The meaning of the title becomes apparent only at the very end of the book.)

The hero of *La Chartreuse de Parme,* Fabrice del Dongo, is again a young man, like Julien Sorel, in fact even younger: he is only sixteen at the beginning of the action. But in all other respects he is very different: the son of a reactionary aristocratic family in northern Italy, he already has social position, money and powerful protection and (consequently, one might say) cares little for these things that were so important to Julien. He is inspired first by the desire for heroism: in the long first sequence he runs away to try to join Napoleon. (The introductory chapter hints that he was in fact the illegitimate son of a young Napoleonic officer of the kind that Stendhal himself had been at the relevant time.) Fabrice makes it to the Battle of Waterloo, but spends the day riding back and forth in confusion until his horse is stolen by real soldiers, when he is taken in charge by a kindly *vivandière*. He is never quite sure whether he has actually taken part in a battle or not. Returning to his family, he is prepared for ordination and a clerical career that holds no attraction for him, and the rest of his life is motivated by passionate love for a virtuous girl, the daughter of a general, who is soon married off to someone else.

Though Fabrice is the youthful protagonist of *La Chartreuse*, he is not central to it in the way Julien is to *Le Rouge et le noir*. Two other characters are at least as important: his thirtyish aunt, Gina Countess Sanseverina, who is in love with him but never tells him so, and her fiftyish lover, Count Mosca, one of the leading political figures at the court of Parma. Much of what happens to Fabrice is the result of intricate plotting by these two figures, intended for his benefit but not always having that result. For long sequences Fabrice is offstage and we learn of the feelings, thoughts and plans of Gina or Mosca, separately or together. Gina acts from a mixture of love and guilt: she has known Fabrice since childhood and feels it shameful that an 'old' woman should be in love with a boy. Mosca knows of her love, though they never speak of it, and protects Fabrice in order to keep Gina close to himself. He too is fond of the boy, but would not be heartbroken if a clerical career removed him from Parma. Mosca's rueful inner monologues make him in many ways the character easiest to sympathize with in the novel: if Fabrice is the dashing boy Stendhal would have loved to be, Mosca, though much more successful than the author in worldly terms, is closer to the middle-aged figure he had become by the time he was writing *La Chartreuse*. Gina, however, is a wonderful, larger-than-life character: beautiful, gifted, generous, able at political intrigue but contemptuous of it, giving her life to passion and stopping at nothing for the sake of the boy she loves.

Clearly this is not a 'realist' novel in the Balzacian mode: the action is roughly contemporary, but it takes place in a small court in Italy where the manners are still those of the eighteenth century and social change seems impossible. In fact, the essentials of the story were taken from a sixteenth-century Italian tale: Stendhal liked to think that the Italian character had changed little since those passionate days, unlike (he thought) the prudish, calculating nineteenth-century French. Italy and love were Stendhal's abiding passions, and his guiding principle the pursuit of happiness. He wrote an essay *De l'Amour* (1822), and his autobiographical writings describe a series of amorous if not always happy attachments. His grave in the Montmartre cemetery bears the epitaph he chose for himself: ARRIGO BEYLE, MILANESE: SCRISSE, AMO, VISSE. Ann. LIX. M. II (Henry Beyle, of Milan: he wrote, he loved, he lived fifty-nine years and two months).

He said that he wrote the *Chartreuse* borne up by enthusiasm for the subject, dictating it in seventy days and sending some pages to the printer in the first, unmodified draft.

We learn this from a letter he wrote to Balzac who, despite the fact that the novel was so unlike his own, gave it an excellent review and thus brought it to an attention it would almost certainly not have enjoyed otherwise. The letter that Stendhal wrote to thank him does not survive, but three drafts of it do. Stendhal's gratitude to the much younger but more successful novelist seems genuine, but he still feels the need to defend himself against the few criticisms that Balzac makes of his mode of writing, and thus we learn a few of his working principles. Stendhal knows that his novels lack elements that many contemporary readers demanded (no descriptions, no tear-jerking emotional effects, no flourishes of style), and says that he does not expect to be appreciated until 1880. This prediction proved to be almost exactly correct.

New interest in his writings in the 1880s led to the publication of two further novels, both unfinished: *Lamiel* (1889, but written in the late 1830s) and *Lucien Leuwen* (1894), and also his *Journal* for the years 1801–18 (published 1888) and two unfinished autobiographical texts, *La Vie de Henri Brulard* (1890) and *Souvenirs d'égotisme* (1892). The plain plaque with its Italian epitaph now appears set into a much more elaborate tombstone, set up by 'SES AMIS DE 1892'.

The Romantics

The first half of the nineteenth century was also, in France as well as in England, the Romantic period. Romanticism was a movement in art and music – some would say also in history, philosophy and even politics – as well as in literature. Literary textbooks used to draw a distinction between Romanticism and Realism, but this quite quickly breaks down. Writers of both 'schools' (which never defined themselves as such) may adopt modern subject matter, and in their choices of form disregard the strict rules of eighteenth-century classicism. Writers described as Romantic place emotion at the very centre of their writing: their heroes' feelings are all-important and the reader is supposed to share these feelings, or at any rate to be awed by them. The Romantic hero typically detests the modern world, and rather than trying to understand and dominate it as Balzac's heroes do, he longs to escape from it in reality or imagination, whether to distant countries or remote historical periods, or even into dreams and madness. Novels, poems and dramas set in Spain, Italy or the Orient, or in the middle ages, were very popular at this time, as were stories of magic, ghosts and demons, the so-called 'contes fantastiques'. Balzac's *La Peau de chagrin*, a tale of magic with an alienated hero, might well be called a Romantic novel, but its realistic and sardonic treatment of the Paris of 1830 takes it far away from Romantic flights of fancy (see Text 11). Again, *La Chartreuse de Parme*, with its Italian setting and plot based entirely on love, has Romantic elements, and Stendhal spoke up for the Romantic movement in *Racine et Shakespeare*; but his humorous treatment of his heroes and heroine, and his plain style, ensured the book's limited success in 1839.

The first great French Romantic was **Francois-René, vicomte de Chateaubriand** (1768–1848), diplomat and politician but also novelist, essayist and historian. His literary celebrity began with *Le Génie du Christianisme* (1802), a four-volume apologia for Christianity based not so much on its truth as on its moral force and its beauty: the beauty of Christian poetry and art. Included in this long work was a short fiction set in the wilds of pre-independence America: *René*. It was soon also published as an independent volume – that is, as a very short novel – and was even more widely read in that form. René is usually thought of as the archetypal Romantic hero in French literature, just as Werther is in German (see Text 11). Also of great interest for its first-hand accounts of the political intrigues of the early nineteenth century, and for its splendid style, is Chateaubriand's multi-volume autobiography. To the composing of this work he devoted the last years of his life, and he chose for it the dramatic title of *Mémoires d'outre-tombe* (Memoirs from Beyond the Grave). It was published immediately after his death, in 1849–50.

TEXT 11 TWO ROMANTIC HEROES CONTEMPLATE DEATH

René, the hero of Chateaubriand's short novel of that name (1805), grows up on a remote country estate, then, as a young man, travels throughout Europe, from Scotland to Sicily, without finding contentment. He finally takes refuge in the wilds of America, where we find him telling his story to a wise tribal elder and a missionary priest:

Le jour, je m'égarais sur de grandes bruyères terminées par des forêts. Qu'il fallait peu de choses à ma rêverie ! Une feuille séchée que le vent chassait devant moi, une cabane dont la fumée s'élevait dans la cime dépouillée des arbres, la mousse qui tremblait au souffle du nord sur le tronc d'un chêne, une roche écartée, un étang désert ou le jonc flétri murmurait ! Le clocher solitaire, s'élevant au loin dans la vallée, a souvent attiré mes regards ; souvent j'ai suivi des yeux les oiseaux de passage qui volaient au-dessus de ma tête. Je me figurais les bords ignorés, les climats lointains ou ils se rendent ; j'aurais voulu être sur leurs ailes. Un secret instinct me tourmentait ; je sentais que je n'étais moi-même qu'un voyageur ; mais une voix du ciel semblait me dire, "Homme, la saison de ta migration n'est pas encore venue ; attends que le vent de la mort se lève, alors tu déploieras ton vol vers ces régions inconnues que ton coeur demande".

"Levez-vous vite, orages désirés, qui devez emporter René dans les espaces d'une autre vie !" Ainsi disant, je marchais à grands pas, le visage enflammé, le vent sifflant dans ma chevelure, ne sentant ni pluie ni frimas, enchanté, tourmenté, et comme possédé par le démon de mon coeur.

[In the daytime, I wandered over great moors bordered by forests. How little was needed to set off my dreaming! A dead leaf blown along in my path, the smoke of a hut rising among the bare tree-tops, a rag of moss fluttering in the north wind on the trunk of an oak tree, a solitary rock, the withered rushes murmuring around a lonely pool! The isolated steeple standing far off in the valley often drew my gaze; often my eyes followed the migrating birds flying above me. I imagined the unknown lands, the distant climes where they are headed, and wished myself borne on their wings. A secret instinct tortured me: I felt that I too was only a traveller, but a voice from heaven seemed to say to me, "O Man, the season of departure is not yet come; wait for the wind of death to rise, then you will spread your wings and take flight for those unknown regions that your heart desires".

"O come quickly, longed-for storms, which will bear René away to the vast spaces of another life". So saying, I strode ahead, my face aflame, my hair streaming in the wind, feeling neither rain nor frost, under a spell, tormented, and like one possessed by the demon in my heart.']

Raphael de Valentin, the hero of Balzac's *La Peau de chagrin* (1831) is, like René, a young aristocrat, and handsome and intellectually brilliant as well. But he is penniless and unknown. In the first scene of the book we see him stake his last coins in a Paris gambling den and lose. Now there is nothing for him, he thinks, but death, and he heads for the Pont Royal.

M. Dacheux was the inspector of the Seine rescue services.

Arrivé au point culminant de la voûte, il regarda l'eau d'un air sinistre.
– Mauvais temps pour se noyer, lui dit en riant une vieille femme vêtue de haillons. – Est-elle sale et froide, la Seine !

Il répondit par un sourire plein de naïveté qui attestait le délire de son courage ; mais il frissonna tout à coup en voyant de loin, sur le port des Tuileries, la baraque surmontée d'un écriteau ou ces paroles sont tracées en lettres hautes d'un pied : SECOURS AUX ASPHYXÍES. M. Dacheux lui apparut armé de sa philanthropie, réveillant et faisant mouvoir ces vertueux avirons qui cassent la tête aux noyés, quand malheureusement ils remontent sur l'eau ; il l'aperçut ameutant les curieux, quêtant un médecin, apprêtant des fumigations ; il lut les doléances écrites entre les joies d'un festin et le sourire d'une danseuse ; il entendit sonner les écus comptés à des bateliers pour sa tête par le préfet de la Seine. Mort, il valait cinquante francs, mais vivant il n'était qu'un homme de talent sans protecteurs, sans amis, sans paillasse, sans tambour, un véritable zéro social, inutile à l'Etat, qui n'en avait aucun souci. Une mort en plein jour lui parut ignoble, il résolut de mourir pendant la nuit, afin de livrer un cadavre indéchiffrable à cette Société qui méconnaissait la grandeur de sa vie. Il continua donc son chemin vers le quai Voltaire en prenant la démarche indolente d'une désoeuvré qui veut tuer le temps.

[Arriving at the top of the span, he looked grimly down at the water.

'Nasty day to jump in', laughed a ragged old woman. 'Cold and dirty, the river, ain't it?'

He smiled back at her, a naive smile that showed all his desperate courage. But he suddenly trembled, seeing at a distance, on the Tuileries bank, the hut with a sign on it in foot-high letters saying HUMANE SOCIETY. In his mind's eye he saw M. Dacheux armed with all his philanthropy, setting in motion the virtuous oars that crack drowning men's skulls if they are unlucky enough to come to the surface. He saw him mustering a crowd, calling for a doctor, preparing a smoke enema; now he read the report of his own sad demise written between the pleasures of a banquet and a dancer's smile; he heard the coins, the price of his head, being counted out to the boatmen by the prefect of the Seine. Dead, he would be worth fifty francs, but alive he was nothing but a man of talent without protectors, without friends, with no one to bang the drum for him, a real social zero, of no use to the State, which cared nothing for him. Death in broad daylight would be contemptible, he decided; he resolved to wait for night, so as to deliver up an undecipherable corpse to the Society that had not recognized the greatness of his life.

So he carried on walking towards the quai Voltaire, with the indolent gait of a man of leisure trying to kill time.]

On the quai Voltaire, Raphael will be offered a choice that transforms his life – but still leads him to death at the end of nine months.

Other French Romantic writers who have continued to be admired and read (though less in recent years than, say, before 1960) are **Alphonse de Lamartine** (1790–1869), lyric poet and in his latter years orator and statesman; **Alfred de Vigny** (1797–1863), poet and dramatist, the author of long philosophical poems and translator of Shakespeare for the French stage (*Le More de Venise,* 1829), **Alfred de Musset** (1810–57), poet, novelist, dramatist and all-round celebrity, and **Gérard de Nerval** (1808–55), poet, critic, traveller, translator of Goethe into French. A series of mental breakdowns from 1841 onwards ended in Nerval's suicide, but he was able to describe his hallucinatory visions with great lucidity in *Aurélia: ou le Rêve et la vie* (1855), and to turn his obsessions into the twelve cryptic but perfect sonnets of *Les Chimères* (1854).

Extremely successful in her day was the novelist who published under the name of **George Sand (**born Amantine-Aurore-Lucile Dupin, 1804–76). Married at 18, a mother at 19, she left her husband after nine years of marriage and soon became notorious for her series of lovers, including Alfred de Musset and Chopin, and for her habit of occasionally wearing men's dress.

She is the exception to the rule that nineteenth-century France, unlike England, had few or no admired women writers.

The *Code civil* of 1804, the new system of laws introduced by Napoleon and little altered despite all the political changes of the ensuing century, placed women in a definitely inferior position, and little was done for their education beyond the rudimentary stage. The new *lycées* were for boys only: the first *lycées* for girls were not opened until 1880. The worlds of writing and publishing were extremely unwelcoming to women: a woman author was seen as something between a monster and a joke. Perhaps Sand was only able to make an initial impact by adopting conventionally male habits. Her early writing, however, passionately takes the woman's part: the heroines of her novels *Valentine* (1831), *Indiana* (1832) and *Lélia* (1833) are beautiful, intelligent, gifted, sensitive women oppressed by the marriage system and husbands who do not understand them. Such novels readily found readers (*Indiana* was a real bestseller), to the disgust and anger of male critics.

By the 1840s George Sand had become a much quieter character (though now involved in left-wing politics) and was writing stories of rural life, some of which remained popular well into the twentieth century, when they came to be regarded as particularly suitable for children. The 'Pantheon Nadar', a huge lithograph produced in 1854 by the caricaturist and pioneer of photography Nadar, nicely shows the respect in which she was held by the mid-century. It brings together caricatures of 249 of the best-known poets, novelists and journalists of the time, in the form of a long winding procession. The great men who had recently died (Balzac, Chateaubriand) are shown as sculpted roundels at the head of the procession. Of the 249 only eleven are women. They are not caricatured: ten of them appear as head-and-shoulders busts placed on a kind of shelf above and towards the back of the procession; they are less than half the size of the

Figure 4 Panthéon Nadar, 1854, detail

most obscure male authors shown, and two of them have their names misspelt. But George Sand, who in her youth had often been caricatured with trousers and cigar, here leads the cortège, in the form of a life-size bust on a pedestal, followed by the main living authors in respectful attitudes (Figure 4).

By the 1860s Sand had become a kind of mother-figure to the world of letters. She had a long, unpatronising correspondence with Flaubert, who addressed her as 'Chère maître', a formula of respect used to older and more successful writers. ('Chère maîtresse' would have been impossible, of course.) His fondness for her did not, however, prevent him from making barbed remarks about her 'feminine' style to his male correspondents.

Hugo

The writer who stands like a colossus above all the Romantics is **Victor Hugo** (1802–85), who in some ways was thought to personify the whole French nineteenth century. This is partly because of the length of his life and the sheer volume of his output, but also because of the number of different genres in which he worked and excelled, and the dramatic life he led outside the realm of literature.

The son of one of Napoleon's generals, Hugo embarked on adult life at seventeen by founding, with his brothers, a literary review. At twenty he was married and had written his first volume of verse. Between 1822 and 1840 he was to publish eight collections of poems, five novels (including *Notre-Dame de Paris*, 1831) and eight plays, set variously in Italy, Spain, France and England at various historical periods. The turbulent first performance of *Hernani* (1830), a verse drama set in sixteenth-century Spain with a high-minded bandit as its hero, is usually taken as marking the triumph of the Romantic drama in France. These unwieldy five-act costume pieces are very rarely revived today, and even at the time the vogue for them was quite short-lived. Hugo's ninth play, *Les Burgraves* (1843), was a resounding failure, which seems to have caused him to turn temporarily away from literature and towards a political career.

By 1845 he was a *pair de France*, a member of the upper house under Louis-Philippe, but he had republican leanings and after the 1848 revolution was elected to the new *Assemblée législative*. Initially sympathetic to Louis-Napoleon on his election as president, Hugo may have hoped for office in his government, but none was offered. Certainly he was enraged by the *coup d'état* of December 1851 and went into exile, first on Jersey and then on Guernsey, where he took a house and remained for nineteen years, firing off satires against the man he now called Napoléon le petit.

When the Second Empire collapsed in 1870, Hugo returned to Paris, to find himself now an almost legendary figure. He was promptly elected to the new *Assemblée nationale* and then to the *Sénat* (the new upper house). Between 1870 and 1885 he wrote a further nine volumes of verse, seven published in his lifetime and two after his death (*L'Art d'être grand-père*, 1877, was particularly popular at the time); a novel (*Quatre-vingt-treize*, 1873, set in the Revolutionary period); another verse drama and a collection of little plays, very free in form (*Le Théâtre en liberté*, 1886). By the time of his death Hugo was regarded as a national hero: his body lay in state under the Arc de Triomphe and then, as he had directed with ostentatious humility in his will, it was borne on a pauper's hearse through the streets of Paris to the Pantheon, resting-place of the country's greatest men. It is said that more than a million people lined the streets to see it go past.

Such a reputation was bound to be deflated by time, and the sad truth is that Hugo is little read today. His larger-than-life stories have provided subjects for operas (Verdi's *Ernani* and

Rigoletto), for films (*The Hunchback of Notre Dame,* seven times filmed; *The Toilers of the Sea,* three times) and, most remarkably, for a hugely successful musical play that was recently staged at the O2 arena in London to celebrate its twenty-five years of continuous performance around the world: *Les Misérables.*

This novel, published in 1862 when Hugo had been living outside France for eleven years, is probably the piece of Hugo's writing that is best known to French people today. Few have read it in its entirety (it is very long and full of digressions), but many have come across it in abridged versions, school extracts and the like. It has been filmed twenty-four times, in various languages, and serialised on television. As a result, some of the characters and elements of the story, like some of Dickens's characters, are known to millions of people who have never read the book. It was a huge publishing success, but privately rather coldly received by writers of the new generation, who disliked its political axe-grinding and found it sentimental and lacking in direct knowledge of contemporary society. 'Il n'est pas permis de peindre si faussement la société quand on est le contemporain de Balzac et de Dickens', Flaubert wrote to a friend. (It is not acceptable to paint society so falsely when one is the contemporary of Balzac and Dickens.) But the younger novelist begins by saying that his remarks must be private, since Hugo is still the revered figure-head of all French writers, the one they had all looked up to in youth. 'Moi [j'ai] passé ma vie à l'adorer', says Flaubert. (I've worshipped him all my life.)

Among Hugo's best writings are the two poetry collections he published in the early years of his exile, *Les Châtiments* (Punishments, 1853), a set of furious diatribes, cast in the most varied poetic forms, against Napoleon III and his regime (see Text 12), and *Les Contemplations* (1856), quieter poems of love and loss written at various times over the preceding thirteen years.

TEXT 12 THE WORST PUNISHMENT

These lines come from Victor Hugo's long poem 'L'Expiation', which was written in December 1852 and published in the collection *Les Châtiments* in 1853. The first three sections show three of the lowest points in the life of Napoleon I: here, the retreat from Moscow, then Waterloo and Saint Helena. Each time the despairing emperor asks God if this is the punishment for his sins, and a mysterious voice replies 'Not yet'. After the return of his ashes to France, and their triumphal reburial in the Invalides, the emperor seems to be at peace, but at the beginning of the last section he awakens in his tomb to find France in the power of a gang of bandits and buffoons all trading on his name: 'Nous sommes les neveux du grand Napoléon!' This is the 'expiation', the real punishment – and for what? The voice replies 'DIX-HUIT BRUMAIRE' – the date of the first of Napoleon's coups d'état.

Il neigeait. On était vaincu par sa conquête.
Pour la première fois l'aigle baissait la tête.
Sombres jours ! L'empereur revenait lentement,
Laissant derrière lui brûler Moscou fumant.
Il neigeait. L'âpre hiver fondait en avalanche.
Après la plaine blanche une autre plaine blanche.
On ne connaissait plus les chefs ni le drapeau.
Hier la grande armée, et maintenant troupeau.
On ne distinguait plus les ailes ni le centre.
Il neigeait. Les blessés s'abritaient dans le ventre
Des chevaux morts ; au seuil des bivouacs désolés
On voyait des clairons à leur poste gelés
Restés debout, en selle et muets, blancs de givre,
Collant leur bouche en pierre aux trompettes de cuivre.
Boulets, mitraille, obus, mêlés aux flocons blancs
Pleuvaient ; les grenadiers, surpris d'être tremblants
Marchaient pensifs, la glace à leur moustache grise.
Il neigeait, il neigeait toujours ! La froide bise
Sifflait ; sur le verglas, dans des lieux inconnus,
On n'avait pas de pain et l'on allait pieds nus.

Ce n'étaient plus des coeurs vivants, des gens de guerre :
C'était un rêve errant dans la brume, un mystère,
Une procession d'ombres sous le ciel noir.
[...]
Toute une armée ainsi dans la nuit se perdait
L'empereur était là, debout, qui regardait.
Il était comme un arbre en proie à la cognée.
Sur ce géant, grandeur jusqu'alors épargnée,
Le malheur, bûcheron sinistre, était monté ;
Et lui, chêne vivant, par la hache insulté,
Tressaillant sous le spectre aux lugubres revanches,
Il regardait tomber autour de lui ses branches.
Chefs, soldats, tous mouraient. Chacun avait son tour.
Tandis qu'environnant sa tente avec amour,
Voyant son ombre aller et venir sur la toile,
Ceux qui restaient, croyant toujours à son étoile,
Accusaient le destin de lèse-majesté,
Lui se sentit soudain dans l'âme épouvanté.
Stupéfait du désastre et ne sachant que croire,
L'empereur se tourna vers Dieu ; l'homme de gloire
Trembla ; Napoleon comprit qu'il expiait
Quelque chose peut-être, et, livide, inquiet,
Devant ses légions sur la neige semées :
Est-ce le châtiment, dit-il, Dieu des armées ?
Alors il s'entendit appeler par son nom
Et quelqu'un qui parlait dans l'ombre lui dit : Non.

[It was snowing. We were defeated by our conquest.
For the first time the eagle was bowing its head.
Dark days! The emperor was returning slowly,
Leaving behind him the smoke of Moscow burning.
It was snowing. The bitter winter was dissolving into an
     avalanche.
After the white plain, another white plain.
No-one could see the leaders or the flag.
Yesterday the Great Army, today a flock of sheep.
The wings could not be distinguished from the centre.

It snowed on. The wounded were sheltering in the bellies
Of the dead horses; outside forlorn bivouacs
Buglers could be seen frozen at their posts,
Still standing, silent, white with frost,
Their stone lips stuck to the brass mouthpieces.
Cannon-balls, bullets, shells, mixed with the white flakes
Were raining down; the grenadiers, surprised to find themselves
    shivering,
Walked pensively on, with ice on their grey moustaches.
And still it snowed and snowed! The icy wind
Whistled; on black ice, in unknown places,
They went hungry and walked barefoot .
They were no longer living hearts, not warriors,
But a dream wandering through the fog, a mystery,
A procession of shadows under the black sky.
An army was disappearing into the night.
The emperor stood watching.
He was like a tree being felled.
Upon this giant, spared until now,
Misfortune, dread woodcutter, had climbed up;
And he, living oak insulted by the axe,
Starting under this ghost with its sinister revenges,
He watched his branches falling all around him.
Chiefs, soldiers, all were dying. Each one had his turn.
And while, lovingly surrounding his tent,
Watching his shadow come and go on the canvas,
Those who were left, still believing in his star,
Were accusing destiny of lese-majesté,
He suddenly felt fear enter his soul.
Stunned by the disaster and not knowing what to believe,
The emperor turned to God: the man of glory
Trembled; Napoleon understood that he was paying the price
For something, perhaps, and, pale and anxious,
Before his legions strewn upon the snow:
'Is this the punishment, O Lord of Hosts?', he asked.
Then he heard a voice calling his name
And someone, speaking out of the darkness, said: No.

What mostly clearly characterizes the writing of the years 1800–50 is a conscious modernity, a feeling in most of the authors that their generations had lived through experiences unprecedented in history, that their society was also evolving into something quite unprecedented, and that their writing should reflect this. The realistic novel is the most lasting expression of this desire for justified novelty.

6

The nineteenth century II: literature for literature's sake

The second half of the nineteenth century was mostly a period of peace and prosperity for the upper and middle classes, despite the Franco-Prussian war of 1870 and the resulting collapse of the Second Empire. During this brief war Paris was besieged for four months, by the end of which time the citizens were eating rats and, famously, had polished off the animals in the zoo. German troops had got as far as Normandy before a peace was negotiated. But political elements of the Paris working class and their left-wing leadership refused to accept the peace terms, and attempted to hold the city with their own forces and run it as a socialist stronghold. This regime, called the Paris Commune, lasted for only two months, from March to May 1871, and ended in a bloodbath, but it has taken on the status of a legend for French left-wingers.

The country at large did not follow the Parisian example, choosing instead to create a Third Republic of largely bourgeois politicians, which was to survive until 1940, the longest-lasting regime between 1790 and 1958. This newfound stability, and the prosperity, at least for some, brought by industrialization and the growth of commerce and finance, greatly increased the market for literature and art. Even among manual workers literacy was increasing (free and compulsory primary education was introduced in 1871), and towards the end of the century novels were being produced in cheaper-than-ever editions and serialized in abridged form in ever more widely distributed daily newspapers.

This expansion of the readership seems to have had the paradoxical effect of making literature more inward looking. Writers, or most of the writers we now admire, turned against the idea of working for a mass public and begin to define literary values in contradistinction to that public's tastes.

The mid-century state could be generous, offering pensions, travel grants, exhibition opportunities and the like to writers and artists who conformed to its ideals, but also imposing censorship on those who did not. When Gustave Flaubert visited Egypt in 1849 with his friend Maxime du Camp, their trip had been partly funded by a government grant, but in 1857 Flaubert found himself before a court of law, charged with outraging public morals by his novel *Madame Bovary*. The same year saw another obscenity trial, that of *Les Fleurs du mal*, by Charles Baudelaire. The two writers had not known each other before their dealings with the courts, but turned out to share some very important ideas about writing. Both works are examples of a new approach to literature: a novel with no explicit 'message', and poems that are not outpourings of feeling with which the reader can readily sympathize. In both writers there is a desire to avoid the obvious and instead to aim at perfection of style. This does not prevent the resulting works from often being intensely moving.

Flaubert

Gustave Flaubert (1821–80) was born and lived most of his life in Normandy, first in Rouen where his father was chief surgeon at the city hospital and where he went to school, and then at Croisset, near the city, where the family had a small estate.

He studied law in Paris in 1840–43, but failed his examinations and, after something resembling an epileptic fit, retired to live at Croisset with his mother and niece and devote himself to writing.

Madame Bovary was his first published novel. It is the story of a young woman, the daughter of a prosperous farmer who has given her a lady's education, sending her to a convent in Rouen. Bored and restless back on the farm, she catches the eye of a young doctor, a simple soul who marries her and takes her to his village practice. Soon bored again (see Text 13), she first has a platonic friendship with a lawyer's clerk, then a full-blown affair with a local squire who soon tires of her, and finally a sexual relationship with the clerk whom she meets again in Rouen. Throughout all this time, unknown to her husband, she has been borrowing more and more money (she is literature's first shopaholic), and when the bailiffs arrive she takes arsenic and, after a protracted and hideous deathbed scene, dies. What gave offence in this story? It was not simply the references to irregular sexual relationships. The French reading public was much less prudish than the English in this regard, and in any case there are no explicit sex scenes in Flaubert's novel (in fact there is a wonderful example of the 'tactful dissolve' in Book I chapter 9, when Emma first gives herself to the squire in a forest glade). Clearly the book was seen by the prosecution as irreligious: the parish priest is shown as well-meaning but deeply stupid, and at the moment of the last rites, the anointing of Emma's body is presented through a series of analogies with her love life. Flaubert's defence lawyer, who secured his acquittal, argued that the book was in fact moral, as it showed an adulterous and spendthrift woman punished in the end. But though Flaubert accepted this defence gambit as necessary, he was not at all happy with it, for by this time he was convinced that works of art should not point explicit morals in this way. In fact his treatment of this case of adultery by a wife is as morally neutral as he can make it.

TEXT 13 DREAMS OF PARIS

Emma Bovary's dissatisfaction with her married life has been crys-
tallised by an unaccustomed invitation to a ball at a neighbouring
château (*Madame Bovary*, I, ix). *La Marjolaine* is a folk-song. Eugène
Sue was an extremely successful writer of serial novels, notably *Les
Mystères de Paris*.

La nuit, quand les mareyeurs, dans leurs charrettes, passaient
sous ses fenêtres en chantant la *Marjolaine*, elle s'éveillait;
et écoutant le bruit des roues ferrées, qui, à la sortie du
pays, s'amortissaient vite sur la terre:
    'Ils y seront demain', se disait-elle.
    Et elle les suivait dans sa pensée, montant et descendant
les côtes, traversant les villages, filant sur la grande route à
la clarté des étoiles. Au bout d'une distance indéterminée,
il se trouvait toujours une place confuse où expirait son rêve.
    Elle s'acheta un plan de Paris, et, du bout de son doigt,
sur la carte, elle faisait des courses dans la capitale. Elle
remontait les boulevards, s'arrêtant à chaque angle, entre
les lignes des rues, devant les carrés blancs qui figuraient les
maisons. Les yeux fatigués à la fin, elle fermait ses paupiè-
res, et elle voyait dans les ténèbres se tordre au vent des
becs de gaz, avec des marchepieds de calèches, qui se
déployaient à grand fracas devant le péristyle des théâtres.
    Elle s'abonna à la *Corbeille*, journal des femmes, et au
Sylphe des Salons. Elle dévorait, sans en rien passer, tous les
comptes rendus de premières représentations, de courses et
de soirées, s'intéressait au début d'une chanteuse, à l'ouver-
ture d'un magasin. Elle savait les modes nouvelles, l'adresse
des bons tailleurs, les jours de Bois ou d'Opéra. Elle étudia,
dans Eugène Sue, les descriptions d'ameublements ; elle lut
Balzac et George Sand, y cherchant des assouvissements
imaginaires pour ses convoitises personnelles.

[At night, when the fish-merchants passed in their carts under her
windows singing *La Marjolaine*, she would wake up; and listening

to the noise of the iron-shod wheels, muted as soon as they reached the dirt road on the edge of the village:

'They'll be there tomorrow', she would think.

And she followed them in her mind, up and down the hills and through the villages, speeding down the toll-road by starlight. At the end of the journey, an indeterminate distance away, there was always a misty place where her dream faded away.

She bought a map of Paris and, tracing the lines with her finger on the paper, would travel around the capital. She would walk up the boulevards, stopping at each corner in front of the white squares that represent the houses. Finally, as her eyes tired, she would shut them and see in the darkness the flames of the gaslights twisting in the wind, and the steps of carriages being lowered with a flourish before the porches of theatres.

She took out a subscription to the *Workbasket*, the ladies' journal, and to the *Drawing-Room Sylph*. She devoured every detail of the accounts of first nights, races and parties, took an interest in a singer's debut or the opening of a new shop. She knew all about the new fashions, the addresses of the best tailors, the fashionable days to be seen at the Bois de Boulogne or the Opera. She read Eugène Sue for the descriptions of room settings, and Balzac and George Sand in search of imaginary fulfilments for her personal yearnings.]

All of the principal characters are treated with some sympathy: Emma, her husband Charles, Léon, the clerk, even the predatory squire Rodolphe, and, however briefly, Justin, the apothecary's apprentice-boy who loves Emma from afar and unwittingly gives her access to the arsenic that kills her. The only exception is M. Homais, his employer, the village apothecary, who is drawn as a personification of everything deplorable in the contemporary bourgeoisie: ambitious, half-educated, sententious, 'progressive' in his ideas and with literary pretensions (he is a member of several corresponding societies

and contributes reports of local events to the Rouen newspaper).
Flaubert's attitude to his characters and their actions is almost
never voiced explicitly: he is the pioneer of the modern method
of fiction writing summed up in the 1920s motto 'Show, don't
tell'. We would never find him saying, like Stendhal in our extract
(Text 10), 'Quelle leçon de morale pour une jeune imprudente !'
(though Stendhal probably has his tongue in his cheek at that
point). Neither does he give the characters inner monologues
('he said to himself', 'she thought') of any length. Instead he uses
two devices to make us privy to their thoughts and feelings, one
of which has been written about at great length, the other less so.
The first is his 'style indirect libre' (free indirect discourse): this
device involves reporting the favoured characters' inner thoughts
in the past tense, which would be used in reported speech, but
omitting the 'he thought', 'she thought'. The reader must ascribe
the ideas to the person who is having them – usually not so
difficult, as at that moment the person in question is often alone,
or lost in his or her own thoughts. The second device involves
putting the reader 'in the character's head', looking out of his or
her eyes or hearing with his or her ears. When we have a lengthy
description in Flaubert, the purpose is rarely historical documentation or sociological analysis as it would be in Balzac: instead the
description is selective, focussing on what a particular character
sees, or rather notices, and dwelling on the elements of, say,
a landscape that are meaningful to that person. A very good
example is the beginning of Book II, chapter 6, when Emma is
looking out of the window on an early spring landscape. Flaubert
describes it in such a way that we come to share her confused
feelings, and understand why she then rushes to the church to
seek spiritual guidance from the hopelessly literal-minded Father
Bournisien.

Neither of these devices is used on M. Homais, who is
presented almost entirely through his speech. He loves the sound
of his own voice, and is always ready with scholarly disquisitions

in comically pompous language, or with ill-timed and ill-chosen advice. He is a creature of words – even his house-front is covered in writing, advertising his wares – and none of them win any sympathy from the reader. Though we may appreciate his comic value, it is a rather sinister kind of comedy.

Flaubert took four years to write *Madame Bovary*, and we can follow almost day by day how he did it. Throughout the process of composition he was writing two or three letters a week either to his mistress Louise Colet or his friend Louis Bouilhet, describing his struggles to achieve the perfect expression he wanted. His drafts for the novel survive and have been published: they are almost ten times the length of the finished text. We see him relentlessly eliminating signs of his own presence in the text, and also anything too obviously comical (except in M. Homais' speeches), though in daily life he loved broad, schoolboy humour. He wrote at this time that 'a novelist in his work should be like God in creation: present everywhere, but nowhere to be seen', and in *Madame Bovary* he comes near to achieving this ideal. Writing as single-mindedly as this, of course, almost demands a private income, which Flaubert was lucky enough to enjoy. For the same reason, he did not have to engage in journalism, which he despised. But he did try, without success, to break into the official theatre by having a play performed at the Comédie-Française, then a route to intellectually respectable fame and fortune.

His next novel was *Salammbo* (1862), which is as unlike *Madame Bovary* as possible, being a highly coloured tale set in ancient Carthage. *L'Education sentimentale* (1869) returns to the recent past, being set at the time of the 1848 revolution. Flaubert described it as 'le portrait moral des hommes de ma génération', and it is rather a cruel portrait, with an indecisive 'hero' who hesitates between four women and in the end loses them all. Set for most of the time in Paris, it has a much broader canvas and larger cast of characters than *Madame Bovary,* but employs some of the same techniques. It was not well reviewed and did not enjoy the 'succès de scandale'of the earlier novel, though some critics nowadays admire it more. It was followed by *La Tentation de Saint Antoine* (1874), a strange, poetical series of monologues by the saint and dialogues between him and various agents of temptation. The subject fascinated Flaubert and he had been working on it on and off since 1845.This final version had some impact on the literary world, but none on the general reader, whom Flaubert finally reached with the last work published in his lifetime, *Trois contes* (1877). These three long-short stories bring together all his preoccupations in writing. The first, 'Un Coeur simple', is an apparently realistic tale set in modern Normandy;'La Légende de Saint Julien l'Hospitalier' a treatment of a medieval legend inspired, he said, by a stained-glass window in Rouen cathedral, and the last, 'Hérodias', a version of the story of the death of John the Baptist . One could think of them all as studies of sainthood in one form or another. Even Félicité, the faithful servant in 'Un Coeur simple', is saintly in her selfless-ness and devotion to others, even if she does end, in old age, by making her devotions to a stuffed parrot! What the three stories have in common is a richness of telling historic or local detail (researched at length in the case of 'Hérodias') and a perfection of style that Flaubert finally attained after a lifetime of struggle.

Much of Flaubert's time in the last years of his life was taken up with research for his last planned novel, *Bouvard et Pécuchet,* which he did not live to complete. It was published after his death, incomplete, in 1881. It is not really a novel as generally understood, but the story of two copying-clerks in search of culture. One of them comes into a legacy, the other realizes his savings, and they decide to retire to the country and master the main fields of human knowledge. They start with science and move to philosophy, religion and education, where they attempt to put into practice Rousseau's ideas in *Emile* by fostering two orphans. Each episode follows the same pattern of hope, enthusiasm, investment in books and equipment, experiment, failure and disillusionment, only to be replaced by enthusiasm for the next new field of study. In this it strangely resembles the *Tiers livre* of Rabelais, a writer whom Flaubert greatly admired. In order to write authoritatively about the various subjects, Flaubert had to research them himself, producing volumes of notes, which still survive. He had said in a letter about his first novel, 'Madame Bovary, c'est moi' (though contradicting this idea entirely in other letters); he could almost equally well have said 'Bouvard et Pécuchet, c'est moi', though the whole undertaking on his part was not underpinned by any faith in the abiding value of what he would discover. His planned ending for the book was that the two clerks should finally decide to return to what they know best – copying – and begin to copy every expression they can find of human wisdom. These were in fact to be the most glaring expressions of contemporary and recent idiocy: old wives' tales, unexamined prejudices and statements of the obvious in pomp-ous language. Flaubert had already begun to collect this kind of material and to copy it with glee into what is sometimes called his 'sottisier' (book of stupid sayings) and sometimes just 'la Copie'. He also delighted in including such 'gems' in his letters to friends. A selection from the 'sottisier' was published as an appendix to *Bouvard et Pécuchet*, and afterwards as an independent slim volume, under the title *Dictionnaire des idées reçues* (Dictionary of Received Ideas).

Of all the nineteenth-century French novelists, Flaubert probably had the greatest influence on modernist writing in French and English and the critical literature on him is enor-mous. New and ever fuller editions of his complete works continue to appear, with his unpublished early stories, letters and working notes now filling more volumes than his published fiction. Jean-Paul Sartre embarked on a psycho-biography of him, which had reached three volumes and more than two thousand pages before Sartre's failing eyesight forced him to abandon it. The title he chose was *L'Idiot de la famille*.

One other important characteristic of Flaubert's characters – apart, of course, from those living in the Middle Ages or ancient Carthage – is that they read: read recent literature and model themselves on it. Admittedly Stendhal's Julien Sorel owned two books, one, given him by an old soldier, a memoir of Napoleon, whom he did take as a role model, and the other an odd volume of *La Nouvelle Héloïse* found in a trunk, which he used as a source of chat-up lines, with an understandable lack of success. But Emma Bovary is a consumer of literature in the modern fashion (see Text 13), and *L'Education sentimentale* is, among many things, a wry parody of the Balzacian story of metropolitan success, with Frédéric Moreau and his friend Deslauriers initially modelling themselves on Balzac's young heroes in their assault upon Paris. This perhaps marks the beginning of a tendency in fiction to be self-reflexive, for writing to be about writing and reading, which we shall see develop much further in the twentieth century.

Baudelaire

Charles Baudelaire (1821–67) was born in Paris, the son of an elderly father who had been educated for the priesthood but left it at the time of the Revolution, and a much younger mother who had lived in England as an *émigrée* in her early years. Old M. Baudelaire died when Charles was six, and for over a year he enjoyed his mother's entire attention. For the rest of his life he was to look back to this time as a period of blissful near-symbiosis. Then his mother married again, to a career army officer called Captain (eventually General) Aupick. Emotionally, Baudelaire seems never to have got over the sense of abandonment caused by his mother's remarriage. A brilliant but wayward teenager, he managed both to come second in the national Latin

verse competition open to all *lycée* students, and to be expelled
from his high school as a bad influence. Living in Paris and nom-
inally studying law, he fell into 'bad company' from which his
parents tried to remove him by sending him on a sea voyage to
the Indian Ocean. However he left the ship at Mauritius and
returned to Paris, where he remained for the rest of his adult life,
apart from brief visits to his mother's houses, first at Neuilly, at
that time still a village, and then at Honfleur, and his ill-fated final
journey to Belgium.

In 1842 he came into his inheritance from his father's will,
and moved to the Ile St-Louis – not so exclusive a neighbour-
hood then as it is now, but still beyond his means, particularly as
he furnished his rooms expensively with pictures and art objects.
His alarmed parents, seeing his capital disappearing, took the
fateful step of giving him a *conseil judiciaire*, that is, of putting his
finances under the control of a lawyer who would pay him a
monthly allowance but not allow him access to the capital. This
was to treat him like a child or a mental incompetent. The allowance was small, and Baudelaire bitterly resented having constantly
to beg the lawyer, a well-meaning soul called Ancelle, for advances.
He lived in this humiliating situation for the rest of his life,
getting deeper and deeper into debt, which he dealt with by
further borrowing. It is not surprising, therefore, that so much of
his surviving correspondence is about money.

Like so many writers of the period, he turned to high-class
journalism, starting in 1845, with a guide to the year's Salon (the
annual exhibition of painting and sculpture). He repeated this in
1846, and also wrote guides to the Fine Art section of the
'Exposition Universelle' of 1855 and the Salon of 1859. Altogether
he published about a dozen articles on painting and sculpture,
including a major essay on Delacroix and one on a now almost
forgotten painter, Constantin Guys, under the title 'Le peintre de
la vie moderne'. This essay has been extremely influential in
defining the notion of modernity in art. A similar number of

essays on writers includes a review-article on 'Madame Bovary' written in late 1857, and a three-part essay, totalling about forty pages, on Edgar Allan Poe, whom he introduced to the French reading public. He was to go on to translate Poe's tales under the title 'Histoires extraordinaires'. His art and literary criticism were collected after his death under the titles 'Curiosités esthétiques' (art) and 'L'Art romantique' (literature). These publications, over a period of about eighteen years, helped to make his name known, but they were not at all lucrative. In 1865 Baudelaire estimated that twenty years of writing and publishing had brought him little more than fifteen thousand francs – about £600 in the money of the day, and pitiful in comparison to his original inheritance of 75,000 francs.

Baudelaire is chiefly remembered today not for his criticism, interesting though that is, but for his poetry, which is still very widely read in France and abroad. He had begun publishing poems in reviews as early as 1843, but it was not until 1857 that they were collected in a single volume, given the title *Les Fleurs du mal* (Flowers of Evil). It was published on 25 June; an extremely hostile review appeared in the *Figaro* on 5 July and on 11 July all copies on sale were seized by the police and the author and publisher charged with outraging public morals. Baudelaire was not so fortunate as Flaubert in his defence counsel, and the pair were fined 300 francs and forbidden to offer the book for sale until six poems, regarded as particularly indecent, had been removed (the curious will find them in the part of a modern edition called 'Les Epaves': two have a lesbian and one a sadistic theme). The result was that the appearance of this collection, which Baudelaire had hoped would bring him some money and public regard, failed on both counts. In 1861 he produced a second edition of *Les Fleurs du mal* with additional poems, which include some of those now considered his best: in particular, with a whole new section called 'Tableaux Parisiens'; a third edition, again with some new poems, appeared after his death in 1868. But his lifetime output of verse – some 160 pieces – is contained in one slim volume: a striking contrast with the most admired poet of the day, Victor Hugo, and his twenty-three collections.

Also in 1857 Baudelaire began to write and publish prose poems – a novel if not wholly unprecedented idea. In the 1830s one Louis Bertrand, self-styled Aloysius, had written a sequence of poems in prose, fanciful pictures of medieval life, which were published the year after his death in 1841 under the title *Gaspard de la nuit* (Ravel was to take them as the point of departure for a suite of piano pieces of the same name). Baudelaire acknowledged Bertrand's influence, but his prose poems are very different: they are all set in modern Paris, and he was planning to publish them under the title *Le Spleen de Paris*: they in fact appeared after his death as *Petits poèmes en prose*.

'Spleen' is an important word for Baudelaire. Much the longest section of *Les Fleurs du mal* is called 'Spleen et idéal', and within it four poems simply have the title 'Spleen'. Looking at these poems will give us an idea of what Baudelaire meant by the word. It is borrowed from English, but does not have any of the connotations of petty spite that we find in expressions like 'vent one's spleen' or 'splenetic'. As Baudelaire uses it, it seems to be an even more extreme form of *ennui*, boredom – and even that was to his mind a vice, the worst of vices. (See the end of 'Au Lecteur' (To the Reader), the introductory poem of *Les Fleurs du mal*.) Spleen is boredom given way to, resulting in anything from a quirky sense of oddity, out-of-jointness ('Spleen' LXXV–LXXVII: see Text 14) to the blackest despair and desire for oblivion ('Spleen' LXXVIII, 'Le Goût du néant'). Giving way to *spleen* means artistic impotence: the artist must pursue *l'idéal*: beauty, energy, goodness. But like the sinner, he lacks grace to follow the good, unless helped by a superior being. This role is played in the collection by a female figure described as an angel, a madonna, a goddess, a muse, sometimes referred to as Baudelaire's 'Vénus blanche' and identified, improbably enough, with a successful demi-mondaine called Madame Sabatier. (Though improbable, the identification is probably correct: several of the 'Vénus blanche' poems were copied out by Baudelaire and sent anonymously to the lady in question.) But such black/white, good/evil distinctions never entirely work with Baudelaire. At least as important in the collection are the poems addressed to a female figure described as dark, a being of night and witchery, whom the poet praises almost as extravagantly as the figure of brightness and redemption. Biographers have identified this figure with the person who was his mistress, despite frequent quarrels, for most of his adult life: Jeanne Duval, a woman of mixed race from the French West Indies whom his friends jokingly referred to as 'la Vénus noire' (an allusion to Sarah Baartman, the famous 'Hottentot Venus' of the early nineteenth century).

TEXT 14 SPLEEN

This poem (number LXXVI of *Les Fleurs du Mal*) is the second in the collection to bear this title. The disjointed couplets of lines 1–8 (the word that completes the rhyme never completes a sentence in the usual way, but sends the mind off in a new direction) contribute a feeling of 'out-of-jointness' that fits the subject. Boucher was an eighteenth-century painter, usually of mildly erotic subjects, whose pictures were often engraved and sold as prints to decorate, particularly, boudoirs.

J'ai plus de souvenirs que si j'avais mille ans.

Un vieux meuble à tiroirs encombré de bilans
Cache moins de secrets que mon triste cerveau.
Je suis une pyramide, un immense caveau
Qui contient plus de morts que la fosse commune.
Je suis un cimetière abhorré de la lune
Où comme des remords se traînent de longs vers

Qui s'acharnent toujours sur mes morts les plus chers.
Je suis un vieux boudoir plein de roses fanées,
Où gît tout un fouillis de robes surannées,
Où les pastels plaintifs et les pâles Boucher,
Seuls, respirent l'odeur d'un flacon débouché.

Rien n'égale en longueur les boîteuses journées
Quand sous les lourds flocons des neigeuses années
L'ennui, fruit de la morne incuriosité
Prend les proportions de l'immortalité.
Désormais tu n'es plus, ô matière vivante,
Qu'un granit entouré d'une vague épouvante
Assoupi dans le fond d'un Sahara brumeux ;
Un vieux sphinx oublié du monde insoucieux,
Oublié sur la carte, et dont l'humeur farouche
Ne chante qu'aux rayons du soleil qui se couche.

[I have more memories than if I were a thousand years old.

A big piece of furniture, a chest of drawers cluttered with balance-sheets, with verses, love-letters, lawsuits, ballads, with heavy locks of hair rolled up in receipted bills, hides fewer secrets than my wretched brain. It is a pyramid, an enormous vault that holds more dead than the paupers' field. I am a graveyard shunned by the moon, where, like fits of remorse, long worms slither and always choose to feed on my dearest dead. I am an old boudoir full of withered roses, where lie disorderly heaps of out-of-date fashions, where the plaintive pastels and faded Bouchers alone breathe in the odour of an unstoppered scent-bottle.

Nothing equals the length of the limping days, when, under the heavy flakes of the snowy years, tedium, born of dull incuriosity, takes on the proportions of immortality. Now you are no longer, O living matter, anything but a block of granite surrounded by a formless fear, lying torpid in the furthest reaches of a misty Sahara; an old sphinx unregarded by the careless world, forgotten on the map, and whose unsociable whim it is to sing only to the rays of the setting sun.]

Other sections of *Les Fleurs du mal* are entitled 'Le Vin', 'Révolte', 'La Mort' and (added in 1861) 'Tableaux parisiens'. These last are all set in the modern city and among its inhabitants, except one, 'Rêve parisien', which describes a city in a (probably drug-induced) dream. Baudelaire is known to have used drugs from 1843 onwards, and in later life to have become addicted to opium, taken in the liquid form of laudanum (see 'La Chambre double' in *Le Spleen de Paris/Petits poèmes en prose*). This was one of the reasons he was later placed by Verlaine among the 'poètes maudits' (poets under a curse).

But it is not the 'accursed' side of Baudelaire that was to make him admired throughout the twentieth century and until today (T. S. Eliot called him 'the greatest exemplar of modern poetry in any language'). It is partly the novelty of his approach. He turns away from the established themes of Romantic poetry: love (requited or unrequited), nostalgia, nature. Asked to contribute to a volume of verse on the theme of Nature, he replied that he had never been able to 'm'attendrir sur les végétaux' (get sentimental about the vegetable kingdom), and submitted the two 'Crépuscule' poems later to appear in 'Tableaux parisiens', which evoke morning and evening twilight in the city in all its harshness. Again, the Romantic poets liked to spread themselves: their poems typically run for several pages, and any images they use are fully worked out and made comprehensible to the reader, whose better feelings are often appealed to. Baudelaire prefers concision and allusion. Understanding him may require the reader to admit to feelings he would rather not recognize: at the end of the prefatory poem to *Les Fleurs du mal*, Baudelaire addresses him as 'Hypocrite lecteur, – mon semblable, – mon frère !' The extracts from Hugo in Text 12, taken from a much longer poem, and the single short poem by Baudelaire printed in this chapter (Text 14) give a good illustration of their differing methods. Nonetheless, Baudelaire admired Hugo and dedicated one of his finest poems, 'Le Cygne', to him. Also of great importance for French readers of Baudelaire is his mastery of sound and rhythm. He composed slowly with many corrections, holding before him – like Flaubert – an ideal of formal beauty, and the patterns of sound in his poems are most intricate and suggestive.

Later poets

The poets of the school immediately following Baudelaire became known as the Parnassians, because they published their verses in an eighteen-part collection called the *Parnasse contemporain*, issued by the publisher Lemerre in 1866, with a subsequent instalment in 1871 and another in 1876. But the name also suggests an aspiration to classical perfection. Their leader, **Charles-Marie-René Leconte de Lisle** (1818–94), in whose house the group used to meet, was in fact three years older than Baudelaire but, like Hugo, lived on into honoured old age. His best-known collections (*Poèmes antiques, Poèmes barbares*) were first published in the 1850s, like *Les Fleurs du mal,* but appeared in later editions, including new material, in the 1870s. The other poets in the group were a generation younger, mostly born around 1840. Like Baudelaire, they wanted to avoid the emotional effusiveness and slack versification of the Romantics and worked to achieve perfection of form, but unlike him they usually achieved these ends at the price of a rather academic-seeming detachment. Their Beauty is, like Baudelaire's, cold and marble-hard ('La Beauté', *Les Fleurs du mal*, XVII), but lacks the flirtatious eyes of his snow-hearted goddess. Nonetheless, these were the officially recognized poets of the day, and school anthologies published up to the Second World War feature their poems at length.

Not only the poets now classed among the Parnassians (Leconte de Lisle, Hérédia, Sully-Prudhomme, Mendès, Coppée) actually published in the *Parnasse contemporain*; it was the main channel, apart from newspapers and magazines, for the publication of new verse. Baudelaire published sixteen 'Nouvelles fleurs du mal' there in the last year of his life and Verlaine and Mallarmé in their youth also did so. Even the provincial schoolboy Rimbaud tried to have his earliest verses published in the *Parnasse*. But these were poets of a very different stamp. They are usually treated together in histories of literature as the Symbolists, but this title has little meaning. It seems to have been chosen for them at the time because their verses were difficult to understand (though in very different ways), and since a literal meaning could not be discerned, it was assumed there must be a hidden, symbolic one.

Stéphane (born Étienne) **Mallarmé** (1842–98) was a *lycée* teacher of English by profession, but by inspiration and decision a man of letters. From his thirties onwards he was in constant contact with 'advanced' movements in writing, painting and music: a friend of Whistler, of Degas and the Manet/Morisot family, of Debussy, and at least an acquaintance of practically every writer of the day. His 'mardis', the famous Tuesday at-homes at his modest flat, were a place of pilgrimage for younger writers for almost twenty years. Having begun everything – schoolteaching, marriage, fatherhood, poetic composition – very early in life (aged 24, he had eleven poems published in the *Parnasse contemporain* of 1866), his output of verse soon became agonizingly slow. Of the 1,300 pages of his collected writings in the standard *Pléiade* edition, which does not include letters, only 180 are of verse and 100 of those are 'vers de circonstance': that is, album and birthday verses, verses accompanying presents, inscriptions on photographs and fans, and versified addresses (twenty pages of these convoluted little quatrains, written on envelopes, which must have provoked the postmen to fury). There are also some fifty pages of prose poems, thirty of which are translations of Poe's verse poems into French prose, and a prose piece described by Mallarmé as a 'conte' (*Igitur*), together with a poem related to it (*Jamais un coup de dés n'abolira le hasard*, No throw of the dice will ever abolish chance), which is in neither verse nor prose, but made up of isolated words and phrases in different typefaces and sizes strewn seemingly at random (but in fact painstakingly placed) across the paper. The rest of the Pléiade volume is made up of occasional prose writing of one kind and another – prefaces to the writings of others, observations on poetry, painting, music and the theatre, even on fashion (Mallarmé was, like Wilde, briefly the editor of a ladies' magazine). All but the earliest are in an elaborate, somewhat precious prose style, which Mallarmé made his trademark. Most of these pieces originally appeared in small-circulation magazines, French, English or American, aimed at the self-defining artistic and literary elite: this was the first great age of 'little magazines'.

A Mallarmé verse poem is typically short or very short (only four are longer than a page, if we include 'Hérodiade', eight pages of a verse drama begun in 1864 but which Mallarme was still talking of completing in the year of his death). His writing is very condensed, often in defiance of normal French syntax, and impossible to paraphrase.

If there is one thing the Symbolist poets have in common, it is the idea that a poem is not a reworking in more elegant terms of something that could be said in plain prose. The story is told of Degas remarking to Mallarmé, 'I should write poems, I have lots of ideas for them', and Mallarmé replying, 'Poems are not made of ideas, M. Degas, but of words'. Similarly, when asked what he had meant (in French, 'voulu dire', wanted to say) by a particular piece of writing, Rimbaud, according to his sister, replied 'J'ai voulu dire ce que ça dit, littéralement et dans tous les sens' (I wanted to say what the thing says, literally and in all possible senses). For the Symbolist poet, a poem is an object, an artefact, to be engaged with on its own terms, and does not come supplied with a satisfying interpretation, by the writer or anyone else. The American modernist Archibald MacLeish was to say something similar in his 1926 poem 'Ars Poetica', which ends 'A poem should not mean/But be'.

MacLeish compares a poem to quite everyday things, natural objects or simple artefacts that we engage with, for example, by touch. Mallarmé's comparison is more ambitious, and drawn from sight. In the essay 'Crise de vers' he speaks of the poet handing over the initiative to the word]s: it is their interaction that will create the poem as they catch light from one another like a pile or necklace of gems: 'comme une virtuelle trainée de feux sur des pierreries' ('Crise de vers', *Pléiade* p. 366).

The poems of **Paul Verlaine** (1844–96) do not burn with a hard gem-like flame. In fact, they often – particularly the most anthologized ones – seem in danger of drifting away like a formless cloud. This imprecision is deliberate. Verlaine too wrote an 'Art poétique', which begins:

> De la musique avant toute chose,
> Et pour cela préfère l'impair
> Plus vague et plus soluble dans l'air,
> Sans rien en lui qui pèse ou qui pose.

> [Music first and foremost
> And to that end, choose the *impair*,
> Vaguer and more easily dissolved in the air
> With nothing in it that weighs heavy or strikes an attitude.]

Traditionally, French verse was written in lines of an even number of syllables, usually eight, ten or twelve (the best-known previous 'Art poétique', Boileau's of 1674, is four cantos of stately alexandrines). The *impair*, the 'odd' line of five, seven or nine syllables, was reserved for 'light' verse, like the fable of La Fontaine in Text 6. So to write an 'Art poétique' in nine quatrains of nine-syllable lines was already a provocation. The rest of the poem, written in a mixture of literary and colloquial language, is a veritable plea for vagueness, lightness and evanescence: like Mallarmé, Verlaine wished to remove any trace of the rhetorical from verse.

In most other respects, their lives and writings could not have been more different. A lazy schoolboy, Verlaine was found an undemanding clerk's job in the Hôtel de Ville, the Paris town hall, and on the strength of that married, aged twenty-six, a girl of seventeen from a respectable family. He had already begun to frequent literary cafés and to write: his first two collections of poetry, now considered to be among his best, appeared in 1866 (*Poèmes saturniens*) and 1869 (*Fêtes galantes*). By 1870 he had begun to drink heavily, and in later life was an alcoholic. In the upheavals of 1871 he lost his job at the Hôtel de Ville, which was burned to the ground, along with other public buildings, in the last days of the Commune. But what had an even greater impact on his life was a fan letter written to him in the same year by a provincial schoolboy seeking to join the Paris literary world. The actual letters exchanged between Rimbaud and Verlaine are lost, but the key words of Verlaine's decisive reply survive: 'Venez, chère grande âme, on vous appelle, on vous attend !' (Come, dear great soul, we call upon you, we are waiting for you).

The boy took him at his word, arriving without money or clothes and expecting Verlaine to look after him. At first the older man took him under his wing, finding him lodgings with literary friends who soon threw him out, and taking him to literary gatherings where many of the guests, even those considering themselves unconventional, were horrified by Rimbaud's language and behaviour, and the evident relationship between the two men. Verlaine's relationship with his young wife and her family had already deteriorated badly, due to his drinking, and after one final, furious quarrel in which he threw his baby son against the wall, he left Paris with Rimbaud first for Brussels and then for London, where many French artists and writers compromised by their association with the Commune were then living. The year 1872–3 was artistically the most productive for both poets, resulting for Verlaine in the collection *Romances sans paroles* (Songs without Words), which is considered his best. But in other respects it was a desperate time of poverty, drunkenness and quarrels, ending in Verlaine's attempt to shoot Rimbaud, for which he stood trial in Belgium and served two years in prison. During that time he returned to the Catholic faith in which he had been baptised, and his next collection, *Sagesse,* expressing penitence and the desire for God's grace, reconciled at least part of the respectable reading public to him.

Alas, his repentance was short-lived, and he led an increasingly disreputable life in England, Belgium and finally in Paris, which included another spell in prison and many more in Paris poor-hospitals, where even the fastidious Mallarmé did not hesitate to visit him. For he continued to publish poetry (nine more collections) and little-magazine journalism and, particularly after the appearance in 1884 of his essays on 'Les Poètes maudits' he was taken up by the younger generation of writers, who elected him 'Prince des poètes' (a purely honorific title) in 1894.

Despite the old joke, Verlaine was not 'always chasing Rimbauds'. He seems never to have wanted to re-enact that terrifying relationship. He had one further long-term relationship with a much younger man, but a gentler character, originally one of his pupils when he was briefly a schoolmaster. Verlaine's sexual relationships in later life seem to have been mostly with women – the kind of women that a bald, penniless alcoholic could hope to attract. Among his later writings are collections of extremely explicit erotic verse (*Les Amies, Femmes, Hombres*), which could not be openly published at the time but are now easily available.

He died in near-squalor in 1896, but Gabriel Fauré played the organ at his funeral service, and Mallarmé spoke at his graveside and wrote a fine sonnet ('Tombeau de Verlaine') on the first anniversary of his death.

Jean-Nicolas-Arthur Rimbaud (1854–91) has no doubt the most extraordinary writing and publishing history of any poet. His father having deserted the family, he was brought up on a small farm outside Charleville in eastern France by his mother, a woman of small education but intelligent, forceful and ambitious for her children. Sent to the Collège de Charleville he was at first considered an outstanding pupil. At fifteen he achieved a distinction in Latin verse in the *concours général* (as Baudelaire had done, but at sixteen, and from the prestigious Collège Louis-le-Grand in Paris), and his teachers had great hopes for him. Alas, at sixteen he 'went off the rails', as teachers say, running away from home, once to Belgium and twice to Paris, the second time during the Commune. Found travelling without a railway ticket, he more than once saw the inside of a jail. From May until September 1871 he was to be seen in Charleville, hanging about in the most disreputable cafes, smoking and drinking beer and cheap wine at the expense (he afterwards said) of older drinkers whom he kept amused with stories of Paris and filthy improvised verses.

But he was also writing: formally conventional poems at first, though from 1870 always on more or less unconventional subjects, and using extraordinary imagery. He obviously hoped to publish these poems and make his mark in the Paris literary world, since he wrote an almost insultingly fulsome fan letter to the established Paris poet Théodore de Banville on 24 May 1871, asking how he might get his work into the *Parnasse contemporain*. Later in the same year he also approached Verlaine, with the results already described. Before leaving, like a Balzacian hero, to take Paris by storm, he wrote out neat copies of all his work to date, and composed one long poem that was to be his showpiece, and which is still considered his greatest: 'Le Bateau ivre'.

'Ivre' (a favourite word with Baudelaire) is very difficult to translate. Its basic meaning is 'drunk' (not 'drunken', which suggests a habit rather than a single experience), but it can also mean exhilarated, intoxicated (with joy, freedom, heroism, love as well as alcohol or drugs). One of Baudelaire's prose poems begins, 'Il faut être toujours ivre' (We must be 'ivre' all the time), and goes on to say 'Mais de quoi ? De vin, de poésie ou de vertu, à votre guise' (But on what? Wine, poetry or [heroic] virtue, as you please). For what it is worth, Rimbaud's boat appears to be drunk on freedom. A trading vessel being hauled along a river, it first escapes the tow ropes and then follows the current into the open sea. Its real 'ivresse' begins once the sea has washed away the signs of everyday drunkenness – stains of cheap wine and vomit – and the boat gives itself up to the power of the waves and the splendour of colour and light. All of these are evoked with hallucinatory vividness by a boy of sixteen who had in fact never seen the sea.

In the 1960s Rimbaud's poems were taken as a tribute to the power of drugs to inspire the artist: drop a tab of acid and you too can write 'Le Bateau ivre'. The results of this method have not been impressive. But in any case, the argument does not stand up historically. Rimbaud wrote all his great early poems before leaving home. Cannabis, in the form of hashish, could be bought in Paris at this time, but probably not in Charleville and certainly not by a boy whose mother doled him out a penny a week to put in the plate in church. Once in Paris he may well have encountered hashish, but for him and Verlaine the intoxicant of choice was always to be the cheapest: bad red wine and industrial absinthe.

By the time of the Brussels shooting, none of Rimbaud's poems had been published, apart from a couple of early pieces, alarmingly competent but conventional in style, in local newspapers. With Verlaine in jail, he retreated to Charleville and there, in his mother's house, wrote *Une Saison en enfer* (A Time in Hell), a group of nine prose poems based on the life he had been leading in the previous two years. Two of these are called

'Délires' I and II: the first one, called 'La Vierge folle', appears to be a reflection on his time with Verlaine, written from the latter's point of view, with Verlaine as the Foolish Virgin and Rimbaud as 'l'Epoux infernal' – the Bridegroom from Hell. The second, 'Alchimie du verbe', describes his poetic ambitions up to that point, which he now seems to be renouncing, and includes eight verse poems composed in 1872–3. It is possible to read *Une Saison en enfer* as an expression of passionate repentance for past folly, and a renunciation of the literary life, and many, particularly Catholic, commentators did read it that way in the early twentieth century. Later critics were able to show, however, that at least some of Rimbaud's collection of prose poems, *Les Illuminations*, were written months or even years later. It was not until 1880, after five years of wandering in Europe, that Rimbaud definitely turned his back on Paris and the friends he had known there and remade his life in East Africa as a trader. Only illness – in the end, insufferable pain – drove him back to France, and he died of bone cancer in a Marseilles hospital in 1891.

TEXT 15 HUNGER

This version of this poem is the one that appears in *Une Saison en enfer.* A different version of the first section appears elsewhere, with the title 'Fêtes de la faim' (Celebrations of hunger). The brook Kedron is mentioned in the Bible.

FAIM
Si j'ai de la faim, ce n'est guère
Que pour la terre et les pierres.
Je déjeune toujours d'air
De roc, de charbons, de fer.

Mes faims, tournez. Paissez, faims,
Le pré des sons.
Attirez le gai venin
Des liserons.

Mangez les cailloux qu'on brise,
Les vieilles pierres d'église ;
Les galets des vieux déluges,
Pains semés dans les vallées grises.

Le loup criait sous les feuilles
En crachant les belles plumes
De son repas de volailles :
Comme lui je me consume.

Les salades, les fruits
N'attendent que la cueillette ;
Mais l'araignée de la haie
Ne mange que les violettes.

Que je dorme ! Que je bouille
Aux autels de Salomon.
Le bouillon court sur la rouille
Et se mêle au Cédron.

[If I feel hunger, it is only for earth and stones. I always lunch on air, rock, coals, iron. Keep turning, my hungers. Feed, hungers, on the meadow of sounds. Draw to yourselves the gay venom of the bindweeds.

Eat the stones the convicts break, the old stones of churches, the pebbles of old deluges, round loaves sown in the grey valleys.

The wolf was crying out under the leaves, as he spat out the fine feathers of his meal of poultry: like him I am eating myself up. Salad leaves, fruit are just waiting to be picked; but the spider in the hedge eats only violets.

Let me sleep! Let me boil on the altars of Solomon. The broth bubbles over on the rust and mingles with the Kedron.]

Meanwhile, Verlaine's essay on him in 'Les Poètes maudits' (1884), illustrated with some of his earlier poems, had won him the notice and praise from young poets that he had so wanted thirteen years earlier. The manuscripts of many of his surviving verse poems were in Verlaine's hands, and he published them at intervals, as well as *Les Illuminations* in their entirety, in the little magazine *La Vogue* in 1886. The story of *Une Saison en enfer* is particularly odd. Obviously realising that it would never find a commercial publisher, Rimbaud had it printed at his own expense in 1873 by a small jobbing printer in Brussels. He took the six free copies he was entitled to and sent four to friends: one copy to the prison where Verlaine was serving his sentence, the others to the young poet Jean Richepin, the artist Forain and Rimbaud's schoolfriend Ernest Delahaye. These were the only copies known until 1901, when the remaining print run of 500 copies was discovered in the printer's storeroom. Unable to pay for the pamphlets, Rimbaud had simply left them behind.

All of his surviving output, therefore, was written between the ages of fifteen and (at the latest) twenty, apart from the memoir of an exploration in the Ogaden desert of Abyssinia; which he sent to the Société de Géographie in 1883. His reputation, however, began to take shape long after he had deliberately renounced writing, continued to grow well into the following century and is still powerful today.

Jules Laforgue (1860–87) died even younger than Rimbaud, at twenty-six, of tuberculosis. But by the time of his death he had produced a large body of verse, which had appeared in two collections, *Les Complaintes* (Street Ballads, 1885) and *L'Imitation de notre-dame la lune* (The Imitation of Our Lady the Moon, 1886). His remaining poems, some of them among his best, were published after his death as *Derniers vers* (1887), as were his parody tales in prose, *Moralités légendaires* (1887). These are rewritings, in a fanciful but satirical style, of stories that Laforgue obviously felt had been overworked by other writers of the time.

The protagonists include Salome (treated by Flaubert in 'Hérodias' and Mallarmé in 'Hérodiade', among many others) and Hamlet (who ends by washing his hands of Elsinore and running off with Kate, the Player King's daughter).

Most of Laforgue's verse poems are similarly light and ironical. Many treat the relations between men and women from the point of view of a young, not very 'masculine' man, who nonetheless is attracted to, if sceptical about, the 'eternal feminine'. (Despite the tongue-in-cheek attitude of these poems, and despite his youth and poverty, Laforgue in fact married an equally young and poor English governess seven months before his death.)

The young T.S. Eliot admired Laforgue and wrote some poems in imitation of him, including two in French. One can still hear some echoes of the Laforgue persona in J. Alfred Prufrock.

Later fiction

Novelists after Flaubert are usually assigned to the Realist or Naturalist schools. These – particularly the latter – were organized movements, with defined membership, recognized leaders and programmes. Realism (the term seems to have been borrowed from the painter Courbet, who first spoke of 'l'art réaliste') was first defined as such after the great realist novelists, Balzac and Stendhal, were dead, with the appearance in 1857 of the manifesto *Le Réalisme* by the comparatively insignificant novelist Champfleury. A Realist novel was to take its subject from everyday contemporary life, reproduced (as if such a thing were possible) with the kind of careful documentation Flaubert had brought to ancient Carthage. The life of the poor was seen as more 'real' than that of the leisured classes (certainly it was a new field for fiction), and the detail in which it was documented led critics to protest at the ugliness and squalor in which, they said, these novelists wallowed. 'Un mot réaliste' came to mean a vulgar or coarse word.

The realists claimed Flaubert as a member of their school, but he angrily rejected this identification. The best realist novels (and even they are hardly a rewarding read) were written by the brothers **Edmond** (1822–96) and **Jules** (1830–70) **de Goncourt,** minor aristocrats living in Paris on a comfortable private income, collectors and critics of art. Needless to say they had no personal experience whatever of low life. Their best-known novel, *Germinie Lacerteux* (1864), was inspired by the distressing discovery that their long-serving maid, whom they imagined to have been solely devoted to cherishing them, had in fact had another life outside their house, taking violent lovers. The Goncourts' novels are little read today: there is much more interest in the their art criticism and particularly in the *Journal* that they began to keep in 1851 and that Edmond continued alone after 1870, which engages readers with its glimpses of literary, artistic and political life and its waspish wit.

Emile Zola (1840–1902), the recognized leader of the Naturalist school, at any rate had had experience of poverty, after the early death of his engineer father and the consequent failure of his business, and later when he was trying to support his mother and establish himself in Paris as a writer. His first proper job was with the Hachette publishing firm, at first in their bookshop but eventually in the publicity department. It was there that he acquired much useful knowledge about book production and promotion. All his novels were serialised in newspapers or magazines and placed in lucrative outlets such as railway bookstalls. He was endlessly productive, of fiction and literary and political journalism, to the point that by 1895 his earnings were estimated at 150,000 francs a year (compare Baudelaire's fifteen thousand over a total of twenty years).

But Zola does not seem to have written chiefly for money. He had a passionate wish to produce a new kind of literature suited to the new scientific age, and attracted around him a group of young disciples who called themselves the Naturalists. Their meetings at Zola's house at Medan are commemorated in a collection of six short stories called *Soirées de Medan* (1880), the most famous of which is 'Boule de suif' (Butterball) by **Guy de Maupassant** (1850–93). After his first big success with *Thérèse Raquin* (1867), Zola conceived the idea of producing, like Balzac, a sequence of novels with recurring characters (Figure 5).

Figure 5 Zola saluting the bust of Balzac, caricature by André Gill, 1878

But unlike the *Comédie humaine*, which had taken shape after the event and to some extent at random, Zola's would be planned in advance, and there would be a necessary connection between all the principal characters, since they would be members, legitimate and illegitimate, of the same extended family. This would allow Zola to show (as he thought) the working-out of heredity and the power of environment in determining human characteristics. The planned series, to be called *Les Rougon-Macquart*, eventually grew from the planned twelve volumes to fifteen and eventually to twenty: still, Zola was able to complete it between 1871 and 1893.

Zola had always been politically active, but from 1894 onwards became particularly involved in the Dreyfus case (the conviction for spying, on forged evidence, of the young Jewish officer Alfred Dreyfus, and the ensuing attempts, over twelve years, to have the verdict overturned). Zola's famous article 'J'accuse', an open letter to the President of the Republic about the case, which occupied the entire front page of *L'Aurore* for 13 January 1898, earned him a year's prison sentence, which he avoided by taking refuge in England. His involvement in this case, and his willingness to risk his own freedom for it, won him many admirers on the left, but an equal number of bitter enemies on the political right. The case inspired such hatred that it has been seriously suggested that Zola's death (at sixty-one, in his home, from carbon monoxide poisoning) was murder.

Of the twenty novels of the Rougon-Macquart series, the most successful at the time and still the most widely read today are *L'Assommoir* (1877), *Nana* (1880) and *Germinal* (1885). All at least begin in a working-class setting, though the heroine Nana goes on to achieve fame and riches as a serially kept woman, one of the notorious creatures who were called at the time the *grandes horizontales* (from the position in which they made their fortunes). The most interesting is probably *L'Assommoir*, the story of a brave, ambitious washerwoman who is eventually brought down by misfortune and drink, for much of it is written in an original style that Zola does not attempt anywhere else. It is a version of Flaubert's *style indirect libre*, but reproducing not only the thoughts of the main character but also those of her neighbours, expressed in the kind of language they might use. Many critics were shocked, not only by the 'low' subject, but also to see Parisian slang and non-standard grammar in print, but Flaubert and Mallarmé both admired the book.

Using the same technique in *Germinal* would not have been an option, however, since to have written it in the dialect of the northern miners among whom it is set would have made it unintelligible to readers in most other parts of France. Instead the style of *Germinal* carries the reader before it with poetic descriptions of beauty and squalor, and stirring set pieces of strikes, demonstrations, mine disasters and the eventual destruction of the mine itself by sabotage. Nothing could be further from the dispassionate, 'scientific' account demanded by Naturalist theory.

Among the Medan group the one who went on to achieve most fame was Maupassant, who soon diverged from the strict Naturalist gospel. His six novels and sixteen collections of short stories show an ironic and even cynical approach to his subjects, and obviously their concise format does not allow for pages of documented description. The stories are perfect of their kind, however, and were models for many writers in England and America. Another early admirer of Zola was **Joris-Karl Huysmans** (1848–1907). His early novels followed the Naturalist precepts (he too was one of the contributors to the *Soirées de Medan*), but after 1882 he began to write in a completely different vein, and his *A rebours* (Against the Grain, 1884), still sometimes read by the determined, is usually quoted as the supreme example of French Decadent writing. It is the 'poisonous French novel' that sets the hero on the wrong path in Wilde's *The Picture of Dorian Gray*.

Des Esseintes, the hero of *A rebours*, is the last scion of a once proud noble house. This was literally true of **Philippe-Auguste, comte de Villiers de l'Isle-Adam** (1838–89), novelist, playwright and writer of short stories, whose ancestors (or so he believed) had fought in the Crusades and been Knights of Malta, but who now lived in wretched poverty in Paris, cohabiting with his laundress, whom he married on his deathbed so as to legitimize his son. Villiers is usually classed as a Symbolist and his lengthy, unstageable dramas probably deserve this title, but his stories, collected as *Contes cruels* (1883), *Tribulat Bonhomet* (1887) and *Nouveaux contes cruels* (1888) are concise and memorable examples of what would later be called 'humour noir'. He also wrote an early science-fiction story, *L'Eve future,* in which Thomas Edison is a character and the Eve of the Future a female android created by him.

Theatre

Having been a centre of political argument and heated rhetoric under the Revolution, the theatre was placed under strict government control during the Empire, and remained so even after its fall. Government approval for the opening of any new theatre was required until 1864, and dramatic censorship was not finally lifted until 1906. Nevertheless, the growth and increased prosperity of the middle class under the Second Empire and Third Republic led to an increase in the number and size of theatres. Paris theatres of 1000-plus seats built at this time and still in use include the Châtelet (1862) and the Théâtres de la Ville, de la Porte Saint-Martin and de la Renaissance, all rebuilt in 1872–3 to replace previous houses burnt down in the last days of the Commune. The state-owned and run Comédie-Française and Odéon continued to present the classics and selected pieces by approved new authors, but audiences for the commercial theatres had more varied tastes. The ceiling of the Châtelet was decorated with cartouches bearing the words *Danse, Opéra, Féerie, Musique, Drame, Tragédie, Comédie, Vaudeville, Pantomime*. A *féerie* was a spectacle-play with elaborate costumes and sets, transformation scenes and the like, rather like the lavish parts of an English Christmas pantomime without the slapstick scenes, whereas a *pantomime* was an all-mimed production. A *vaudeville* was, and is, what English speakers call a French farce: a complicated story of misunderstandings, mistaken identities, hiding in cupboards and so forth, with a comic plot usually based on one or more attempted adulteries. The great, late master of *vaudeville* was **Georges Feydeau** (1862–1921). Comedies in this vein but somewhat less frantic are also called *comédies de boulevard*: this, because commercial theatres were originally situated mostly on the Paris boulevards, first on the Boulevard du Temple but later on the new wide roads cut through the city by Baron Haussman in his renovations of 1852–70. 'Boulevard theatre' is therefore an expression like 'Broadway' or 'Shaftesbury Avenue' theatre. A *drame* might be any kind of non-comic play in prose. Opera and light opera in its various forms (*opéra-comique, opéra-bouffe, opérette* – they are not very clearly distinguished) were also extremely popular with the middle-class public. Here the great name is that of **Jacques** (born Jacob) **Offenbach** (1819–80), the son of a German cantor who settled in Paris and took French nationality. His sparkling *opéras-bouffes*, the best of them written to libretti by Meilhac and Halévy, held the stage from 1858 until 1870, and are thought to be the best embodiment of the pleasure-loving spirit of the upper classes under the Second Empire. Also put on in the large theatres were lavish costume-dramas, of which **Sarah Bernhardt** (1845–1923) was the best-known exponent. Her influence in the theatre was enormous, not only as an actress but also as a commissioner of new plays and, from 1893, the manager of her own company, first at the Théâtre de la Renaissance and then, from 1899, at the Théâtre Sarah-Bernhardt on the Place du Châtelet. This house was renamed Théâtre de la Cité in 1940 when the Nazis insisted on the removal of the Jewish actress's name, and is now the Théâtre de la Ville.

Such were the tastes of the broad mass of theatre-goers. But just as in prose writing and poetry, there was another kind of theatre appealing to the more intellectually inclined. Companies of actors would open up in small premises and put on work by little-known or foreign dramatists, often using acting styles and set designs very different from those of the established theatres. The most successful of these undertakings were the Théâtre Libre, led by André Antoine, and the Théâtre de l'Œuvre, led by the actor Lugné-Poë.

The Théâtre Libre opened in the unfashionable 18th *arrondissement* in 1887 and apart from mounting foreign work by such dramatists as Ibsen and Strindberg, specialized in 'slice-of-life' plays by the Naturalist school, with realistic sets to match – an early example of 'kitchen-sink' drama. Just as the Impressionist school in painting had originally emerged from the *salon des refusés* of Imperial times, so the Théâtre Libre declared its mission was to show the work of the 'refusés de la Comédie-Française et de l'Odéon'. It failed in its original premises in 1894, and the name Théâtre Libre passed to a successor company, so that when Antoine was able to put his together again in 1897 he had to rent a new theatre, on the Boulevard de Strasbourg, and rename it the Théâtre Antoine. In 2011, it was still functioning there, with fairly ambitious programming.

The Théâtre de l'Œuvre operated in a small off-street theatre from 1893 to 1899, also offering Ibsen and Strindberg, but otherwise specialising in Symbolist dramas (including Wilde's *Salome* in 1896). Perhaps its best-remembered piece of programming was not Symbolist, however, but rather the unclassifiable *Ubu Roi* (Ubu the King) (1896) of the eccentric poet **Alfred Jarry** (1873–1907). This bloodthirsty farce begins as a kind of wild parody of *Macbeth* but continues as a grotesque satire of modern diplomatic and tax-raising methods. It was played in wholly unrealistic style in hand-painted costumes and masks, and had a *succès de scandale* not matched by its sequels *Ubu cocu* (Ubu Cuckolded) and *Ubu enchaîné* (Ubu Bound, which, despite its title, is not a parody of *Prometheus Bound*, but more of a satire *per absurdum* of French Third-Republic ideals of freedom and equality). Jarry's plays have given the French language the word *ubuesque,* meaning overweening, ignorant, irrational, violent but at the same time absurdly comical. The late Emperor Bokassa, for example, was often referred to (in private) as a *personnage ubuesque.*

These little theatres and others like them had a huge influence on the development of drama in France and other countries in the twentieth century. But it was a boulevard entertainment that was really to revolutionize the public's experience of fiction. On 28 December 1895, at the Grand Café, 14 boulevard des Capucines, the Lumière brothers gave the first public showing of their *cinématographe.*

7

The twentieth century: the age of transgression

One of the most admired French writers of the late nineteenth and early twentieth centuries was **François Coppée** (1842–1908). François who? Exactly. The author of thirteen collections of poetry, seventeen performed plays, many of them at the Comédie-Française (Sarah Bernhardt made her debut in his *Le Passant)* and six volumes of assorted prose, mostly autobiographical, Coppée is now completely forgotten. It would be safe to say that more people in a year now read the seven brief parodies of his verse written, and no doubt forgotten, by the seventeen-year-old Rimbaud than anything by Coppée himself.

To begin to understand why, we could read the entry on him in the *Encyclopedia Britannica* for 1911. The author says that Coppée 'concerned himself with the plainest expressions of human emotion, with elemental patriotism, with the joy of young love and the pitifulness (*sic*) of the poor, bringing to each a singular gift of sympathy and insight' (in his lifetime in France he was known as 'le poète des humbles'). The author admits that Coppée can be sentimental and even trivial, but ends his appreciation with the words, 'by neglecting that canon of contemporary art which would reduce the deepest tragedies of life to mere subjects for dissection' (he means Naturalism) '[Coppée] won those common suffrages that are the prize of exquisite literature'.

Rimbaud wrote his verses in the autograph book of a disorderly dining club calling itself the Cercle Zutiste (*Zut*, a word that is meaningless but considered vulgar, is an expression either of annoyance or, as probably here, defiance). The album contains parodies and obscene rhymes and drawings by various members of the club, including Verlaine. The entire book (*Album zutique)* was published in facsimile in 1962. Rimbaud's parodies are cruelly accurate imitations of Coppée's manner, all but one in his preferred form, the *dixain* (poem of ten lines), and on such 'humble' subjects as a lavatory brush, a *pissoir* or a sex manual. He cannot have imagined that they would ever see the light of day. But twentieth-century readers, at any rate those considering themselves readers of 'literature', came to look down upon 'plain expressions of human emotion' (let alone patriotism of the Coppée sort – he was a virulent supporter of the anti-Dreyfus party), and instead to admire transgression, whether in life or art.

Half a century of war

The twentieth century was, for France, the century of two further invasions by Germany. The first of these led to a four-year war in which a million and a half Frenchmen died, as well as more than a million British Empire and Dominion troops and a hundred thousand Americans. (The figures for Frenchmen include some eighty thousand colonial troops who either volunteered or were drafted to fight for the mother country. Having lost her first empire in the eighteenth century, France had acquired another in the later nineteenth and early twentieth, before losing it again slowly and painfully in the 1950s.) The 1914–18 war was to have been, everyone hoped, 'The War to End Wars', in soldiers' parlance 'la der des ders' (*dernière des dernières,* last of the last). Yet by 1938 it was becoming clear that war was on the way again, and in September 1939 it broke out. Having struck a secret deal with Soviet Russia, Hitler invaded Poland, which Britain and France had sworn to defend. But nothing happened (except to the Poles) for a few months, until in May 1940 German troops rolled with terrifying speed through the Netherlands, Luxembourg and Belgium, heading for the French frontier. The French army, badly led and depleted by 1914–18, could not withstand the onslaught, and in June 1940, with 100,000 men already killed and two million taken prisoner, the French government sued for peace. An armistice was signed on 22 June and a new regime was put in place, led, from Vichy in central France, by the eighty-four-year-old Marshal Pétain, revered hero of the 1914–18 war. The Germans occupied the north of France, leaving the south as a so-called *zone libre*, which stayed free, of course, only so long as the Vichy regime followed German orders. In 1942 German direct rule was extended to the whole of France. By this time an active resistance movement of men and women was secretly at work in many parts of the country, and a nucleus of soldiers and airmen who had managed to escape to Britain, either directly or via the colonies not occupied by the Germans, had joined the Free French forces led from London by General de Gaulle. These forces fought bravely alongside the much more numerous British and American armies after D-Day, and were allowed the symbolic victory of being the first Allied troops to enter Paris on 25 August 1944.

These two great wars, especially the First, naturally gave rise to a great deal of writing. As most of France was not occupied in the First World War, patriotic literature aimed at the home front could be and was published and sold in great quantity. Little of that writing is now read or even remembered. The only 'First World War Poet' writing in French who is still widely read is **Guillaume Apollinaire** (born Wilhelm Apollinaris de Kostrowitsky, 1880–1918), a Paris-based Pole who fought with the French army from 1914, received a serious head wound in

1916, which did not completely stop him writing, and died in the worldwide influenza epidemic of 1918. His most important collections are *Alcools* (1913), poetry written between 1898 and the year of publication, and *Calligrammes* (1918), which includes his poetry written in the trenches between 1914 and 1916, but also much poetry on other topics, particularly love (many of the 'war' poems are also love poems). The 'calligrammes' of the title are a score of visual poems, where the letters of the text are set out in the form of pictures related to the title. In 'Il pleut', for example, they are trickling down the page like rain down a window. Apollinaire was a close friend of many of the Cubist painters, and along with other art journalism published essays on their work in *Les Peintres cubistes* (1913).

The period 1895 to 1914 is often referred to as 'la Belle Epoque' (the Good Time), a nostalgic phrase that came into use during the First World War. The years 1918 to 1931 (from the Armistice to the Great Depression) are called 'les Années Folles' – the Crazy Years. This was a time when France admitted foreign – chiefly American – cultural influences to a degree never seen before. The cinema had been invented in France, and French companies, notably Pathé and Gaumont, had played an important part in its early development. But the power of American capital (put together to a large extent by recent immigrants from Europe) and the year-round sunlight of California were too much for any European national industry to compete with, and by the end of the First World War, Charlie Chaplin, Mary Pickford and Tom Mix were international cultural icons. American troops stationed in France had brought ragtime and jazz with them, and soon French youth was dancing 'le one-step' and later 'le charleston'. The emblematic figure of 'les Années Folles' is Josephine Baker, the nineteen-year-old Afro-American dancer who came to Paris in 1925 to appear in the 'Revue Nègre' (*sic*) and stayed to become a star of French music hall and in due course a resistance worker decorated with the *Légion d'honneur.*

Dress, and social life in general, became much more relaxed in the 1920s. If one watches a French film of this period it is striking that whereas the middle-aged and elderly men still look Victorian, with dark clothes, starched high collars, waxed moustaches and/or beards, the young men are clean shaven, with soft collars and lighter, looser fitting clothes, while the young women have bobbed hair and – most shocking – knee-length skirts. The impact on the older generation – particularly those who had lost sons in the War – was considerable. **Simone de Beauvoir** (1908–86) in her *Mémoires d'une jeune fille rangée* (Memoirs of a Well-Behaved Girl, 1958) gives a good account of growing up as the daughter of an upper-middle-class family at this period of change.

Surrealism

The literary movement most associated with the 1920s is Surrealism, which of course was not purely a literary movement: Surrealists were active in painting (Dalí, Miró, Max Ernst, Magritte) and the cinema (Buñuel), and refused to recognize boundaries between the arts, or indeed between art and the chance occurrences of life. The leading French Surrealist poets were **Pierre Reverdy** (born 1889) and the somewhat younger group of **Louis Aragon** (also a novelist), **André Breton**, **Paul Eluard** and **Philippe Soupault**, all born between 1895 and 1897. The Surrealists sought total freedom, from bourgeois social conventions and traditional artistic forms, but strangely enough attempted to found an organized movement with manifestoes, group discipline, expulsions and so forth. One is reminded of Jarry's *Ubu enchaîné,* in which the Free Men meet daily for Freedom Drill, forming ranks to disobey the orders of their corporal. In fact Jarry was one of the earlier writers the Surrealists most admired and saw as their forerunner, along with Baudelaire, Nerval,

Rimbaud and the self-styled **Comte de Lautréamont**, born Isidore Ducasse (1846–70), a nineteenth-century failed student who had his wild prose poems (*Les Chants de Maldoror*) printed at his own expense in 1868, followed by *Poésies* (also in prose) shortly before his death in 1870. (These writings remained perfectly unknown to the literary or any other world until a Belgian little magazine published some extracts from *Maldoror* in 1885, and some symbolists, including Jarry, began to take notice of them). What all these writers have in common is being what Verlaine called 'poètes maudits' (poets under a curse): unconventional in their behaviour (in Nerval's case to the point of periodic clinical insanity) and in their writings; pursuing altered states of consciousness and dying young: Nerval at 47 by suicide, Baudelaire at 46, probably of tertiary syphilis, Rimbaud at 37 of cancer after a life of privations in the East African deserts, Jarry at 34 of meningitis after years of alcoholism, Lautréamont at 24, probably of tuberculosis, but little is known of his life. There is something to be said for the idea that Surrealism was the last gasp of Romanticism. (It would perhaps be cynical to note that most of the Surrealists lived to a ripe old age: Aragon to 85, Soupault to 93, Breton to a more modest 70 and Dalí to 85, the latter two having sat out the Second World War in New York).

The Surrealists wished to break the control of the conscious mind, rationality and the superego (this was the time when Freud's ideas were becoming current among intellectuals), and to set free the power of the unconscious. One way they tried to do this was by 'automatic writing': sitting down in front of the paper and managing to make one's mind a complete blank, so that the hand moved independently of conscious control, producing texts that, they hoped, would surprise the author as much as any eventual reader. Texts produced by this and other methods (some strangely like English pencil-and-paper games such as 'Consequences') were shared within the group. But most texts published by the Surrealist writers were produced by more conventional means.

One of their favoured themes was the very Romantic one of 'amour fou': wild, unreasoning love, often provoked by a stranger. Surrealist poets made heavy use of imagery, the more spontaneous and incongruous the better: Breton defined surrealism in poetry thus: 'le vice appelé surréalisme consiste en l'emploi déréglé et passionnel du stupéfiant image' (the vice called surrealism consists of the unbridled, passionate use of the drug imagery). They loved incongruity in general: it was Max Ernst who first made fanciful, sometimes unnerving collages (much imitated in later years) by cutting and pasting unrelated images from old illustrated books – sometimes commercial catalogues. They despised the established institution called 'literature': the title of their magazine *Littérature* (Figure 6) was ironically intended. A definition of the beautiful much quoted by surrealists came from Lautréamont's *Chants de Maldoror*: 'beau comme la rencontre fortuite sur une table de dissection d'une machine à coudre et d'un parapluie' (beautiful as the chance encounter on a dissecting table of a sewing machine and an umbrella). In the original, this wild simile, along with others equally bizarre, is applied to the blond English boy being stalked by the monster-hero.

In politics, the Surrealists were drawn towards the extremes: mostly to the left, and an important part of the history of the Surrealist movement, indeed of French literature in general until about 1970, concerns its relations with national and international communism. The French Communist Party was formed in 1920 by splitting off from the then Socialist party. Communists and Surrealists shared little beyond their hostility to the bourgeoisie, since the Party stressed duty and discipline and indeed enjoined rather a strait-laced lifestyle on its members. Nonetheless it recruited energetically among artists and writers between the wars and also after 1944, when it had managed to consign Stalin's wartime pact with Hitler to the memory hole and was enjoying its largest

Figure 6 *Littérature*, a Surrealist review, cover by Francis Picabia, 1923

ever following among the electorate (twenty-eight per cent of the vote in 1946, the highest of any political party). Throughout the 1940s and 1950s it was supported by industrial workers, but also by many self-defined intellectuals, school and university teachers as well as writers. Despite Hungary, Czechoslovakia and even the fall of the Berlin Wall, it staggered on, controlled and funded by Moscow until the nineties, still attracting ten per cent of the vote in 1997. It can now count on between two and five per cent.

Novelists

Notable prose writers of the first half of the twentieth century – all transgressive in their own ways – were **André Gide** (1869–1951, Nobel Prize for Literature 1947), **Marcel Proust** (1871–1922) and, a lesser but interesting figure, **Jean Cocteau** (1889–1963).

Gide's first publications in fact belong to the 1890s (as a very young man he attended some of Mallarmé's 'mardis'), and some of his best fiction was written before the First World War, notably *L'Immoraliste* (1902), *La Porte étroite* (1909) and *Les Caves du Vatican* (1914). He did not give the title *roman* (novel) to any of these works, calling the first two *récits* (accounts) and the third a *sotie* (sixteenth-century term for a satirical play acted by fools). What they all have in common is that they are workings-out in fictional terms of aspects of his own life, which was a complicated one. The son of a respected protestant professor of law (Protestants in France are a formerly persecuted and therefore somewhat defensive minority), but spending school holidays with Catholic relatives, he was at first attracted by an almost mystical Catholicism personified by his cousin Madeleine, whom after years of courtship he eventually persuaded to marry him in 1895. The marriage was never consummated, however, since a journey to North Africa in 1893–94 had revealed to him his homosexuality – to be more precise, his attraction to young boys. The fraught relationships that resulted obviously furnish the plot of *L'Immoraliste,* which is a brief first-person narrative of almost eighteenth-century clarity, told by Michel (the guilt-ridden yet defiant husband) to a group of his friends, one of whom establishes the frame-story. Michel is an unreliable narrator: we cannot always take his word for everything that happened, or for his feelings at various points. Gide did not invent the device of the unreliable narrator: he acknowledges his debt to, for instance, the Scottish novelist James Hogg, author of the *Confessions of a Justified Sinner* (1824). But he used it so effectively as to make it distinctively his own. In a similar way, the situation of the central figure of *La Porte étroite* (Strait is the Gate), Alissa, is very close to that of Madeleine before her marriage. The story is told mostly through letters and diary entries, which again have to be carefully read to try to tease out an understanding of the characters' real feelings for each other.

After the anguish of these *récits*, *Les Caves du Vatican*, a much longer, deliberately complicated tale told in the third person, offers more relaxed comedy. The unlikely plot – about a confidence trickster attempting to swindle money out of French Catholics with the story that the Pope has been kidnapped and is being held prisoner in the Vatican cellars of the title – involves three middle-aged brothers-in-law, each of whom seems to represent one aspect of Gide's own character at some stage of his life to that point: the pious and sexually naive Amédée Fleurissoire, the aggressive freethinker Anthime Armand-Dubois and the successful novelist Julius de Baraglioul. All are sent on wild goose chases across Europe by the actions of the conman Protos and of the fourth male relative – a much younger illegitimate half-brother of Julius named Lafcadio Wluiki who, on the spur of the moment, murders poor Amédée by pushing him out of a train (see Text 16). This was the first and most notorious example in fiction of what would later be called the 'acte gratuit' (motiveless action). If the brothers–in–law all embody partial aspects of what Gide was, Lafcadio is the perfect ideal of everything he was not but would dearly have loved to be: young, irresistibly handsome, mercifully free of family, sexually polymorphous without guilt, and capable of spontaneous action, for good or ill, without thought of motives or consequences.

TEXT 16 WHAT NOW?

An important value for Gide was what he called 'disponibilité': the fact of being 'available' to new experiences, not set in one's ways. In *Les Caves du Vatican*, from which this extract comes (Livre V, opening pages), the 'disponible' characters call themselves 'les subtils', as opposed to 'les crustacés', the middle-aged characters set in hard shells or exoskeletons of habit. The 'il' of the first line is Lafcadio, the young hero recently come in to an inheritance.

Tout seul dans le wagon qui l'éloignait de Rome, il respirait le bien-être par tous ses pores ; le cou non serré dans un col presque haut mais peu empesé, d'où s'échappait, mince comme un orvet, une cravate en foulard bronzé, sur la chemise à plis. Il se sentait bien dans sa peau, bien dans ses vêtements, bien dans ses bottes – de souples mocassins taillés dans le même daim que ses gants ; dans cette prison molle, son pied se tendait, se cambrait, se sentait vivre. Son chapeau de castor, rabattu sur ses yeux, le séparait du paysage ; il fumait une pipette de genièvre et abandonnait ses pensées à leur mouvement naturel.

La vieille, avec un petit nuage blanc au-dessus de sa tête et qui me le montrait en disant : la pluie, ce ne sera pas encore pour aujourd'hui ! ... cette vieille dont j'ai chargé le sac sur mes épaules (par fantaisie il avait fait à pied, en quatre jours, la traverse des Apennins entre Bologne et

Florence, couchant à Covigliajo) et que j'ai embrassée en haut de la côte ... ça fait partie de ce que le curé de Covigliajo appelle les bonnes actions, – je l'aurais tout aussi bien serrée à la gorge – d'une main qui ne tremble pas – quand j'ai senti cette sale peau ridée sous mon doigt ... Ah, comme elle caressait le col de ma veste, pour en enlever la poussière! en disant : *figlio mio! carino!* D'où me venait cette intense joie quand, après et encore en sueur, à l'ombre de ce grand châtaignier, et pourtant sans fumer, je me suis étendu sur la mousse ? Je me sentais d'étreinte assez large pour embrasser l'entière humanité ; ou l'étrangler peut-être ... Que peu de chose la vie humaine ! Et que je risquerais la mienne agilement, si seulement s'offrait quelque belle prouesse un peu joliment téméraire à oser ! ... Je ne peux tout de même pas me faire alpiniste ou aviateur ...

[Alone in the train compartment taking him away from Rome, he was breathing out well-being from every pore. His neck was gently held in a fairly high but not starched collar, from which a bronze-coloured silk tie, slim as a slow-worm, snaked across across his pleated shirt-front. He felt at home in his skin, at home in his clothes, at home in his boots – soft mocassins cut from the same suede as his gloves. In that supple prison his foot could move, stretch, feel itself alive. His soft hat, pulled down over his eyes, cut him off from the surrounding landscape. He was smoking a little juniper-wood pipe and letting his thoughts follow their natural drift. He thought:

'The old woman with a little white cloud over her head that she pointed to and said "It will rain, but not today" ... I carried her backpack for her (on a whim he had walked across the Apennines from Bologna to Florence, taking four days on the way and sleeping at Covigliaio) and kissed her goodbye at the top of the climb... what the priest at Covigliaio would call a good deed, I expect – I could just as well have gripped her throat when I felt that horrible wrinkled skin under my fingers ... How she stroked the collar of my jacket when she was brushing the dust off it, saying "There you are, son! Bless you!" ... Why did I feel that tremendous elation

> when, still sweating from the climb and without even smoking, I lay down on the grass under that huge chestnut tree? I felt my arms wide enough to embrace the whole of humanity – or to strangle it, perhaps. What a small thing human life is! And how promptly I'd risk mine, if only there were some appealingly rash feat to risk it for! ... I can hardly become a mountaineer or an aviator ...]

Gide's fictions found more readers, and his moral principles (strict honesty in the free pursuit of one's individual fulfilment) more followers after the First World War than they had before. In 1924 he decided to publish *Corydon*, a set of Socratic dialogues in defence of homosexuality, which he had been working on since 1910, but which previously had circulated only among his trusted friends. The scandal this caused was only intensified by the appearance two years later of *Si le grain ne meurt* (If It Die), an account of his childhood and early adolescence. Sexual reminiscences in fact play only a small part in this study of a developing consciousness but, as if determined to shock, Gide devotes his second paragraph to a brief description of his four-year-old self playing with his willy under the dining-room table, in the company of another little boy similarly engaged. Shining in his angel-infancy this was not, and readers of 1926 responded with foreseeable outrage. The year before, Gide had published *Les Faux-Monnayeurs* (The Counterfeiters), the only one of his fictions to which he was willing to give the name of *roman*. It is indeed a complex, carefully worked-out story involving characters of several families and generations, from schoolboys to their grandparents. The central figure is a middle-aged novelist called Edouard, who narrates more than half of the story. He has an intense curiosity about the lives of much younger people, mostly boys and young men, though his interest in them is at first not overtly sexual. Rather, he involves himself in their lives and influences their decisions, usually for the worse. He is writing a novel to be called *Les Faux-Monnayeurs*, and many of his diary entries relate to the writing process. Just to make complication complete, Gide himself was keeping a diary while writing this novel, and it was also published the following year under the title *Journal des Faux-Monnayeurs*.

A prolific writer of fiction and essays, Gide also had an active public life. A keen traveller, he published accounts of his journeys, which involved him in political dispute, whether anti-colonial (*Voyage au Congo,* 1927, and *Le Retour du Tchad*, 1928) or with supporters of communism. He had gone to Russia as a sympathetic fellow-traveller, but what he saw there disillusioned him entirely, and his *Retour de l'URSS* (1936) made him *persona non grata* with the French Communist Party, then very influential among intellectuals. Indeed, all his life he seems to have thrived on controversy.

He was also one of the founders, in 1909, of the *Nouvelle Revue Française*, which was the leading literary journal throughout the inter-war period and still appears as a quarterly today. In the capacity of reader for the NRF he had the doubtful distinction of turning down *Du côté de chez Swann,* the first part of what was to become the life-work of Marcel Proust (Gide came to regret the decision and later apologized for it: Proust joined the NRF stable in 1916).

Proust

Marcel Proust (1871–1922) is probably the twentieth-century French novelist whose name has been most familiar to English-speaking readers since the 1950s. (The 1970s comedy series *Monty Python's Flying Circus* even included a game-show sketch in which contestants had to 'Summarise Proust [mispronounced Prowst] in Twenty Seconds'.) He was the son (like Flaubert) of a respected and successful doctor, while his mother was the daughter of a convert Jewish banking family. Brought up a Catholic, Proust was conscious of his Jewish ancestry: he could hardly have failed to be so, since the Dreyfus affair was raging throughout his middle and late twenties. He signed the first intellectuals' petition for a retrial, in 1898, thereby closing many houses to himself: a sacrifice he must have felt, since in his early youth he had been ambitious for acceptance in aristocratic as well as artistic society.

After 1905, in increasingly poor health, he turned away from the fashionable world to devote himself entirely to writing. He had already written a thousand pages of notes for a novel about a young man's entry into upper-class society and into the worlds of art and politics. These notes were eventually put into an order by editors and published in 1952 under the title *Jean Santeuil* (the name of the hero, who is obviously very closely based on the author himself). But Proust was clearly not satisfied with them, since he began the whole work again, this time narrating it in the first person. His first plan was for a work in two volumes, then in three, but as he kept writing, the text kept expanding until, with the addition of the parts written but not yet published at the time of his death in 1922, it reached a total of seven volumes and more than three thousand pages. The complete work, entitled *A la recherche du temps perdu* (In Search of Lost Time), broke almost all the unspoken rules of how a novel should be composed. There is a single central character, whom Proust called 'le monsieur qui dit je' (the gentleman who says 'I') and who he insisted should not be identified with himself despite the similarities in many of their experiences. The narration does follow a rough historical sequence, in the sense that the first part of the first volume, 'Combray', is set in the narrator's childhood in the 1880s (though few precise dates are ever given), and the last, 'Le Temps retrouvé' (Finding Time Again) takes us to the years immediately after the First World War. But within every volume reminiscences constantly take us backwards and forwards in time, often within a single page, and the story – to the extent that there is one – is lost sight of in pages of reflection on art, literature or music. But as the subject is the narrator's slowly developing understanding of these things, as well as of love, ambition and the deception of others and oneself, nothing can be dismissed as irrelevant.

Proust's determination to grasp everything by writing about it leads him to develop elaborate similes and compose some immensely long, convoluted sentences: the most notorious lasts for a page and a half, though it is broken up by semi-colons. None of this makes for easy reading, and when Proust attempted to publish his first volume, *Du côté de chez Swann* (The Way by Swann's) in 1912 it met with a series of rejections and was eventually published at the author's expense. (One commercial publisher's reader reported that 'I felt I was going insane'.) The book had an unexpected success with the reading public, how-ever, and was taken up by the NRF and republished by them in 1916 and 1919. All subsequent volumes were published by the NRF or, later, the publisher associated with them, Gallimard.

Part of the book's attraction no doubt lay, and still lies, in Proust's sharp sense of social comedy, whether he finds it in the old-fashioned household and village of Combray or in the aris-tocratic and artistic social milieux that the narrator joins as a young adult. Intense and intellectually challenging, this is also often an extremely funny book. Readers daunted by the thought of 3,000 pages of text could well begin with the middle part of *Du coté de chez Swann,* called 'Un amour de Swann' (Swann in Love), which is often printed as a separate paperback of 200 pages or so. The story of a love affair, told in the third person, past tense and rarely interrupted historical sequence, it is much more like a conventional novel than anything else in Proust, but is still a good introduction to his style and humour.

Unlike most of the writers discussed in this chapter, Proust had nothing to do with any political or artistic movement later than the Dreyfus case. Though he is now classed as a Modernist, he never used the word and probably had little idea of the thing. He was inspired more by the music of Debussy and the painting of Monet than by any contemporary French writer, and the nineteenth-century writers he admired, apart from Flaubert and Balzac, were mostly foreign: Dostoevsky, Ruskin, Dickens, Hardy. He never took a public stance as a homosexual, though his orientation was well known to his friends, or as a Jew, though Charles Swann, one of the most sympathetic characters in the novel, is a Jew of a convert family like Proust's mother's, and the latter part of the novel is a series of revelations, some quite surprising, of homosexuality in a succession of the male characters: never, however, in the narrator, who falls in love with a series of young women. Gide regarded this artistic decision as cowardice on Proust's part, but Proust believed that his duty was to write, and not to try to bring about social change.

TEXT 17 THE TRIGGERING OF A MEMORY

Proust has just explained, at the beginning of *Du côté de chez Swann*, how he used to spend sleepless night hours deliberately recalling certain events and settings of his early life at Combray. But then, one day, his mother gave him a piece of madeleine (a small, plain cake tasting something like Madeira cake) to dip in lime-flower tea. Suddenly he had a sense of intense pleasure – happiness – joy that he could not explain (his failure to explain is described over two and a half pages), until he remembered that this was the taste of the madeleine his Aunt Leonie (now long dead) used to give him at home on Sunday mornings. Suddenly the whole of his childhood comes rushing back, and becomes the subject of the first section of this first volume.

Et dès que j'eus reconnu le goût du morceau de madeleine trempé dans le tilleul que me donnait ma tante (quoique je ne susse pas encore et dusse remettre à bien plus tard de découvrir pourquoi de souvenir me rendait si heureux), aussitôt la vieille maison grise sur la rue, où était sa chambre, vint comme un décor de théâtre s'appliquer au petit pavillon donnant sur le jardin, qu'on avait construit pour mes parents sus ses derrières (ce pan tronqué que seul j'avais revu jusque-là) ; et avec la maison, la ville, depuis le matin jusqu'au soir et par tous les temps, la Place où on m'envoyait avant déjeuner, les rues où j'allais faire des courses, les chemins qu'on prenait si le temps était beau. Et comme dans ce jeu où les Japonais s'amusent à tremper dans un bol de porcelaine rempli d'eau, de petits morceaux de papier jusque-là indistincts qui, à peine y sont-ils plongés, s'étirent, se contournent, se colorent, se différencient, deviennent des fleurs, des maisons, des personnages consistants et reconnaissables, de même maintenant toutes les fleurs de notre jardin et du parc de M. Swann, et les nymphéas de la Vivonne, et les bonnes gens du village et leurs petits logis et l'église et tout Combray et ses environs, tout cela qui prend forme et solidité, est sorti, ville et jardins, de ma tasse de thé.

[And as soon as I recognized the taste of the crumb of madeleine dipped in lime-flower tea that my aunt used to give me (even though I did not yet know and was not to learn until much later the reason why the memory made me so happy), all at once the old grey house on the street loomed up like a piece of stage scenery and attached itself to the little annexe looking onto the garden that had been built on to the back wall for my parents (the only part of the house that I had recalled up to then), and along with the house, the town, from morning to night and in all weathers, the square where I was sent to walk before lunch, the streets where I did errands, the paths where we took walks if the weather was fine. And as in that game the Japanese play, of putting in a porcelain bowl filled with water, little balls of paper that, as soon as they are dropped in, begin to stretch, turn about, take on different colours and shapes to become flowers, houses or three-dimensional, recognizable people, so now all the flowers in our garden and in M. Swann's park, and the waterlilies in the Vivonne and the village people and their little houses and the church and all of Combray and its surroundings, all of these things taking on shape and solidity, streets, houses and gardens, came out of my cup of tea.]

Jean Cocteau (1889–1963) would be considered a light-weight compared to Gide, Proust or the Surrealists, partly because he worked in so many different media and genres: verse, prose, drama, criticism of literature and music, but also drawing and printmaking, film (as scriptwriter and/or director), and as librettist for operas and writer of scenarios for ballets. In the vanguard of every fashion, he is cruelly caricatured in Gide's *Les Faux-Monnayeurs* under the name of the Comte de Passavant, a fame-seeking, sexually exploitative artistic fraud. But he has left at least one excellent novel, *Les Enfants terribles* (1929) and a beautiful film, *La Belle et la bête* (Beauty and the Beast, 1945), which is still to be found showing somewhere in Paris practically every month of the year. His distinctive drawings are also often to be seen in card shops alongside those of Picasso and Matisse.

The Second World War and after

The literature of the Second World War was of necessity very different from that of the First. Not that the Germans tried to suppress French culture entirely: some of the officer class admired it and could speak the language well. Indeed, France was promised an honoured place as a purveyor of culture in the new, German-ruled Europe. The entertainment industry – theatre, opera and operetta and cinema – continued to flourish as the large cities, and particularly Paris, became rest-and-recreation bases for German troops, with theatres and nightclubs for the officers, and commandeered cinemas showing German films for the other ranks. But the French-language film industry also prospered despite German censorship. Many of the leading actors and directors had stayed in Paris and some excellent films were made at this time. Some were costume subjects, like *Madame Sans-Gêne* (1941) or *Les Enfants du paradis* (1943), others apparently contemporary, but in the latter it was forbidden to mention the war or its consequences for civilians like rationing, and street scenes might not include passing German troops or the ubiquitous German-language notices. Films therefore offered a temporary escape from everyday life under occupation, and cinemas were packed every night, not least because no fuel was available to heat homes. Theatres too, from the Comédie-Française downwards, continued to function, their Jewish managers sidelined where necessary, and some important new plays were performed, including Sartre's *Les Mouches* (The Flies, 1943) and *Huis clos* (In Camera/No Exit, 1944), the first set in ancient Thebes and the second in Hell.

Novels, plays and poems treating the war realistically or supporting the resistance could obviously not be published openly, but some were issued by underground presses printing in small workshops and distributing clandestinely. The best-known of these is Les Editions de Minuit, which went public at the Liberation and remains successful today. After the war it published Samuel Beckett and all the 'nouveau roman' writers (whom we shall consider later), as well as two highly influential essays on the Algerian war, which were censored in their turn. The first publication of the Editions de Minuit was *Le Silence de la mer*, published in 1942 under the name of Vercors by Jean Bruller, one of the founders of the press. It is still quite often set as a schoolbook, both for French children and foreign learners, since it is short, not too gory and written in fairly simple language. Despite taking the side of the resistance it contains quite a sympathetic portrayal of a young German officer.

The period immediately following the war was a confused time in many ways. Suddenly everyone had been a resistant, apart from a few writers whose collaboration with the Nazis had been too blatant to be ignored. The most notable of these was **Louis-Ferdinand Céline** (born Destouches, 1894–1961), who had served in the trenches and been wounded in the First World War and later qualified as a doctor, travelled to Africa and the US, and practised medicine in a poor district of Paris. He used these experiences as the point of departure for a remarkable novel, *Voyage au bout de la nuit* (Journey to the End of Night, 1932). Set chiefly in the slums of Paris, the book also takes its hero, a doctor like the author, to Africa, New York and Detroit. Despite the book's low-life subject, its exaggeration, black humour and highly coloured, invective-laden style make it entirely unlike a Naturalist 'slice of life'. Many of the scenes portrayed are indeed horrible, but for those with the strength to persevere it is a truly memorable read.

Given the narrator's contempt for authority, for colonialism and American capitalism and his feeling for the sufferings of the poor, one might imagine that the writer would have had sympathy for left-wing ideas. Indeed he accepted an invitation to the Soviet Union in 1936. But on his return he published a pamphlet, *Mea culpa,* expressing his horror at the Soviet system. From then on, his anarchic impulses took him in the opposite direction, towards fascism. Long before the German invasion he published three vile anti-Semitic pamphlets, as crude in their language as their ideas. So it was not surprising that he welcomed the arrival of the Nazis and became an enthusiastic collaborationist. Fearing for his life after the Allied victory, he fled with the survivors of the Vichy government first to Germany and then to Denmark, where he was first imprisoned and then remained in exile until 1951. On his return, living in poverty in a Paris suburb, he was not able to begin publishing new work until 1957, when a three-part novelised treatment of his life in exile began to appear. Since his death in 1961 he has slowly come to be recognized as the great and original writer he undoubtedly was. But how to reconcile a brilliant style with a contemptible set of political ideas and actions is a problem that French students of literature are still wrestling with.

In the political sphere, the immediate post-war years were marked by a competition for power between pre-war politicians hoping to pick up from where they had left off, Gaullists associated with the Free French army, whose legitimacy was recognized by the victorious Allies, and the French Communist Party, which considered that it had played the main part in organizing resistance from within the country. A new Republic (the Fourth) was proclaimed in 1946, but the power struggles continued.

A further aftermath of the war was the growth of independence movements in France's colonies. The French colony of Indo-China had remained under the nominal control of the Vichy regime, though in fact under the power of Japan, until March 1945, when Japan took open control. After the defeat of Japan, Laos and Cambodia secured their independence, but France decided to try to regain and hold Vietnam. A long guerrilla war ensued, ending in the disastrous encirclement and defeat of the French forces at Diên Biên Phu in 1954. Soon after that the country was divided and France gave up her claims. But by 1955 America had taken over France's role of fighting the Communists in the North, and for the next twenty years Indo-China became part of US rather than French history. No sooner had the Indo-China War ended than war flared up in Algeria. Both wars had a strong impact in metropolitan France, not least because (like the American Vietnam War) they were fought by armies of conscripts (draftees). But the impact of the Algerian War was more direct and stronger, since Algeria is much nearer to France and many more people of European descent were settled there. Every expedient was used to hold on to Algeria but without success, and finally General de Gaulle, who had returned to power in 1958 with the support of the army and the settlers, to their fury recognized the inevitable and gave Algeria her independence in 1962. By that time retreat from the French colonies in Africa had already been peacefully secured, on terms that allowed France to retain her financial interests and cultural dominance there.

Existentialism

During the late 1940s and early 1950s one intellectual and literary movement was dominant in France: existentialism. This began as a philosophical school of which the acknowledged leader was **Jean-Paul Sartre** (1905–80). Trained as a teacher of philosophy (which all French *lycée* students are required to take for the baccalaureate), Sartre was seconded to the French Institute in Berlin in 1933–4. This allowed him to deepen his knowledge of the classic German philosopher Hegel (1770–1831), but also of his living successors Husserl (1859–1938) and Heidegger (1889–1976). The philosophical approach of the latter two started from human consciousness and experience (rather than abstract theories), and laid great stress on human beings' ability and obligation to make choices in the conduct of their lives. These are ideas that Sartre developed in his own writings. For him, the mere fact of being a live human being requires us constantly to make choices, and it is the choices we make that determine the person we are. The very idea of 'a good person who somehow keeps doing bad things' would be nonsense to Sartre. He does not use the terms 'good' or 'bad' much, but for him no-one can be 'essentially good' as no one is 'essentially' anything: each of us decides each day what person he or she is going to be. Most people, he thinks, fear this freedom and use various devices to hide from it: this strategy he calls 'mauvaise foi' (usually translated as 'bad faith: the everyday meaning of the phrase is simply 'dishonesty'). 'Mauvaise foi', an extremely important concept in Sartre's moral philosophy and fiction, is avoidance of responsibility: pretending that one was not free to have behaved otherwise than one did in the past, or will not be free to choose one's actions in the future. Such behaviour is clearly not peculiar to twentieth-century people, and one can find striking illustrations of it in much earlier literature: Molière's Tartuffe protesting that he has to act as he does because the interests of heaven demand it (Act IV sc.1), or Racine's Pyrrhus saying he accepted betrothal to Hermione because of duty ('Je suivais mon devoir', Text 5). 'Mauvaise foi' may take the form of appeals to religion, for example ('I have to do this because my faith requires it'), or to social convention ('What would people say?'), or to one's 'nature' ('That's the way I am'), one's upbringing or one's genes. Sartre did not believe in 'nature' in this sense, and the attempt to explain human behaviour by genes had not really got under way while his failing eyesight still allowed him to read. Obviously no one is wholly free from material constraints – we cannot suddenly decide to fly out of the window, or even to take a plane if we have no money. But Sartre's bracing view is that we are all much freer than we like to think, and spend too much of our time finding pretexts to deny our freedom.

Other wrong directions people take are when they choose to exist in the eyes of others (*pour autrui*) rather than for themselves, in their own freedom (*pour soi*), or when they try to take on the permanence and 'essential' character of inanimate things, which exist *en soi* (in themselves), as the young Lucien does in Text 18. Human beings cannot do this, but must always remain 'contingent', fluid rather than defined. These and other Sartrian ideas are put to work in human situations in his fiction (the short novel *La Nausée* (Nausea, 1938), the collection of short stories *Le Mur* (The Wall, 1939) and the long novel sequence *Les Chemins de la liberté* (Roads to Freedom, 1945–9), and in his plays, especially *Huis clos* (In Camera/No Exit, 1944) and *Les Mains sales* (Dirty Hands, 1948). A late and particularly revealing piece of work is his childhood autobiography *Les Mots* (Words, 1964), in which many of his ideas are shown to have their origins in the life and learning experiences of an unusually intelligent, fatherless only child of the Parisian upper bourgeoisie.

TEXT 18 SELF-DISCOVERY?

Lucien, the central character of Sartre's short story 'L'Enfance d'un chef' (Childhood of a leader) is the only son of a factory owner, who has always known that he will be expected to succeed his father and in his turn become a 'leader of men'. We see the boy first as a small child, then as an older child and here as a teenager. He is always looking for someone else to tell him who and what he is – a mistaken quest, according to Sartre, since no one *is* irrevocably anything. Here Lucien has taken a Surrealist as mentor. The ensuing scene is a striking portrayal of what is now called 'grooming'. 'Les assis' is the title of an early poem by Rimbaud.

– Savez-vous, Lucien, comment j'appelle votre état? Lucien regarda Bergère avec espoir : il ne fut pas déçu.

– Je l'appelle, dit Bergère, le Désarroi.

Désarroi : le mot avait commencé tendre et blanc comme un clair de lune, mais le 'oi' final avait l'éclat cuivré d'un cor.

– Désarroi …, dit Lucien.

Il se sentait grave et inquiet comme lorsqu'il avait dit à Riri qu'il était somnambule. Le bar était sombre, mais la porte s'ouvrait toute grande sur la rue, sur le lumineux brouillard blond de printemps ; sous le parfum soigné que dégageait Bergère, Lucien percevait la lourde odeur de la salle obscure, une odeur de vin rouge et de bois humide.

'Désarroi …', pensait-il : 'à quoi est-ce que ça va m'engager?' Il ne savait pas bien si on lui avait découvert une dignité ou une maladie nouvelle : il voyait près de ses yeux les lèvres agiles de Bergère qui voilaient et dévoilaient sans répit l'éclat d'une dent d'or.

– J'aime les êtres qui sont en désarroi, disait Bergère, et je trouve que vous avez une chance extraordinaire. Car cela vous a été donné. Vous voyez tous ces porcs ? Ce sont des assis. Il faudrait les donner aux fourmis rouges, pour les asticoter un peu. Vous savez ce qu'elles font, ces consciencieuses bestioles ?

– Elles mangent de l'homme, dit Lucien.

– Oui, elles débarrassent les squelettes de leur viande humaine.

– Je vois, dit Lucien. Et il ajouta – Et moi? Qu'est-ce qu'il faut que je fasse?

– Rien, pour l'amour de Dieu, dit Bergère avec un effarement comique. – Et surtout ne pas vous asseoir, à moins, dit-il en riant, que ce ne soit sur un pal. Avez-vous lu Rimbaud?

– Nnnon, dit Lucien.

– Je vous prêterai *Les Illuminations.*

Jean-Paul Sartre, *Le Mur* © Éditions GALLIMARD

['Do you know what I call your state, Lucien?'

Lucien looked at Bergère hopefully: he would not be disappointed.

'I call it Désarroi [confusion, distress, being at a loss]', said Bergère.

'Désarroi…', said Lucien.

He felt solemn and uneasy, like the time he had told Riri he was a sleepwalker. The bar was dark, but the door was wide open onto the street, on the luminous blond mist of spring; underlying the expensive scent that Bergère wore, Lucien could pick up the heavy smell of the dark room, a mixture of red wine and damp wood. 'Désarroi', he was thinking. 'What does that let me in for?' He wasn't sure if he'd acquired a new distinction or been diagnosed with a new disease: before his eyes, Bergère's agile lips were constantly hiding and revealing the glint of a gold tooth.

'I like people who are "en désarroi", Bergère was saying. 'I think you're extremely lucky. It's a gift you've been given. Look at all those pigs. Those are "assis", people who live sitting down. We ought to give them to the red ants, to liven them up a bit. You know what those busy little creatures do?'

'They eat people', said Lucien.

'Yes, they clear skeletons of their human meat'.

'I see', said Lucien, and he added, 'And what about me? What should I do?'

> 'Nothing, for God's sake', said Bergère with a look of comic horror. 'Above all, don't sit down – unless it's on a stake', he added, laughing. 'Have you read Rimbaud?
> 'N-n-no' said Lucien.
> 'I'll lend you *Les Illuminations*'.]

All of Sartre's fictional works are clearly and accessibly written: the plays, indeed, are constructed on conventional, 'boulevard' lines, and, apart from *Les Mouches*, had considerable success in the commercial theatre. Sartre's philosophical writings are a very different matter. His first and most successful work, *L'Etre et le Néant* (Being and Nothingness, 1943) is readable with determination: the section on 'mauvaise foi' is perhaps the most accessible. But all the later philosophical works are definitely for professionals only – and professionals within his own philosophical school.

Sartre's worst legacy to his country has been his decision to invent his own philosophical vocabulary, forming new words on basically German principles ('l'être-là', the fact of being there, from German 'Dasein' would be a very simple example). Traditionally, French writers had always aimed at clarity. In 1674 Boileau had told aspiring authors that

Ce que l'on conçoit bien s'énonce clairement
Et les mots pour le dire arrivent aisément

[What has been thought through properly will be voiced
    clearly
And the words to express it will arrive easily]

and generations of French schoolchildren were made to learn the couplet by heart, along with the 1784 dictum of Antoine de

Rivarol (in fact Rivaroli, an Italian), 'Ce qui n'est pas clair n'est pas français' (If it's not clear, it's not French). All but the most impeccable school answers would come back with one or more red ink comments in the margin: 'pas clair'. But by the 1960s the ideal of clarity was regarded as oppressive, if not fascistic; following Sartre's example, every self-respecting theorist had to invent a personal terminology and, it sometimes seems, write as cryptically as he or she could manage.

Other notable writers of the existentialist school, broadly defined, are **Simone de Beauvoir** (1908–86), the lifelong companion and intellectual and political ally of Sartre, and **Albert Camus** (1913–60), a wartime ally of Sartre and de Beauvoir who later quarrelled with them and refused the 'existentialist' label.

De Beauvoir, also a professional teacher of philosophy, was certainly the intellectual equal of Sartre (she came second to him in the fearsome *agrégation* exam, the top qualification for teachers, despite being three years younger), yet in their lifetime she seems to have been content, despite her feminism, to remain in his shadow. Her groundbreaking feminist work *Le Deuxième sexe* (The Second Sex, 1949) is still widely read and has had a great influence, no doubt partly because she was content to write it in ordinary French, without creating her own terminology. She also wrote several novels and, starting in 1958, a series of autobiographical texts that eventually ran to six volumes, the last (*La cérémonie des adieux*) concerned with the physical decline, last illness and death of Sartre. On her own death six years later she was buried next to him.

Camus was not a professional philosopher but a working journalist. His father was killed in the First World War and he was brought up in great poverty by his profoundly deaf mother in the then French city of Algiers. A primary-school teacher spotted his talent and got him the scholarship that let him go to *lycée* and from there to the University of Algiers. But there was no money for postgraduate study and hence no *agrégation*: Camus had to go to work to keep his mother and himself. (The teacher remained his lifelong friend and Camus dedicated his Nobel Prize acceptance speech to him.) In view of all this it is not surprising that his novels and his two philosophical essays (which would not be accepted by professional philosophers as contributing to their discipline) are less theoretical and more down to earth than those of Sartre. For Camus, our main philosophical and moral task is to face up to the absurdity of life. Our life is absurd (in his sense) because it must end in death: it has no intrinsic meaning. We can try to hide from this truth by pretending that it does, by taking refuge in religion or patriotism or social convention (this is very like Sartre's idea of 'mauvaise foi'), but the Absurd will not go away. What we have to do is look it in the face and then commit ourselves to a human life. Any value our life can have will be the value we ourselves can give it. This notion of commitment (*engagement*) is common to all the existentialist writers, and for that reason their writing is sometimes called 'littérature engagée'. For Camus, *engagement* first took the form of working for the wartime resistance, and then of involving himself in the Algerian war, speaking out first against the oppression of the Muslim population, but then against the terror tactics of the Liberation Front and in defence of the mass of European settlers, the *pieds-noirs*, literally 'black-feet'. They were so called because, in legend at least, many of them had arrived in the country barefoot, fleeing desperate poverty in the south of France or Spain, and many, like his own family, were still poor and struggling. By these attempts to see the complicated situation honestly, Camus managed to alienate both sides and to quarrel with most of the Paris intellectual world. His life was threatened and when he was killed in a car crash in 1960 there were, as with Zola, rumours (probably false) of murder.

Camus wrote three novels, of which *L'Etranger* (The Outsider/ The Stranger, 1942) is probably the best known, though *La Peste* (The Plague, 1947) was also very successful. Of his four plays

Caligula (1938, first performed 1945), about the Roman emperor, is the one most often revived.

A figure very difficult to fit into any formal history of literature is the novelist and playwright **Jean Genet** (1910–86). A bastard orphan, fostered out in childhood, he had no formal education beyond the village school (where he excelled), and by his late adolescence was a thief and male prostitute, spending long periods in reformatory and prison, followed by a brief spell in the Foreign Legion. Nonetheless he wrote an elegant and even fastidious French, quite unlike the 'tough-guy' English into which some of his novels have been translated. His themes of homosexual love in criminal and prison milieux attracted the attention of Cocteau and Sartre, who helped him to have his first novels published. Sartre regarded him as an existentialist hero and prefaced Genet's first collected works with a long essay, originally published anonymously, called 'Saint Genet, comédien et martyr' (St Genet, actor and martyr: the title was borrowed from a play by the seventeeth-century playwright Jean Rotrou about a Roman actor martyred for his Christian beliefs).

By the late 1940s existentialism had become a fashion, first in France and soon around the world, reaching even Japan. There were existentialist hangouts, cafés in the daytime and jazz cellars at night, and an existentialist look (cropped or very long hair for girls, pale faces with lots of eye make-up, sloppy sweaters preferably in black, capri pants or circular skirts, ballerina slippers – think Juliette Gréco or Audrey Hepburn in 'Funny Face' – and for boys general dishevelment, a look of not having slept for days). The world centre of existentialism-as-fashion was the Left-bank district of Saint-Germain-des-Prés in Paris, then a centre for small publishers, booksellers and art galleries, now for expensive clothes and interior design shops. The emblematic figure of the old Saint-Germain-des-Prés was **Boris Vian** (1920–59), engineer, jazz trumpeter, singer/songwriter, novelist, dramatist and poet. Though he was a friend of Sartre and De Beauvoir, his best novel, the fantastical-tragical *L'Ecume des jours* (1946) includes a caricatured account of a lecture given by 'Jean-Sol Partre' with the 'Duchesse de Bovouard' in attendance, which is overwhelmed by hordes of their unruly fans.

Theatre

In small theatres in the same 'existentialist' orbit, plays of a new kind were soon being put on, which were given the name of 'théâtre de l'absurde' by the German critic Martin Esslin in 1962. The title did not please all the dramatists, and indeed their plays owe less to the existentialist notion of the Absurd, as developed by Camus, than to pre-war experimental theatre like Apollinaire's *Les Mamelles de Tiresias* (The Dugs of Tiresias, 1917, called by its author a 'drame sur-réaliste', the first appearance of this term), or the Surrealist Roger Vitrac's *Victor: ou les Enfants au pouvoir* (Victor, or Power to the Children, 1929). In these plays there is much spectacle and humour, but no consistent plot or character-ization: the characters speak and behave absurdly, in the everyday sense of the word, and the effect is to undermine and ridicule 'bourgeois' common sense and consistency.

The early plays of **Eugène Ionesco** (born Ionescu, 1909–94; Romanians have always had difficulty in France with the final syllable of their names) very much follow this pattern. His *La Cantatrice chauve* (The Bald Prima-Donna) is set in the drawing-room of an English (so obviously laughable) couple called the Smiths, who are visited by their friends the Martins. Their stilted dialogue, made up of non-sequiturs, was inspired, as Ionesco himself admitted, by the Méthode Assimil (the French equivalent of Linguaphone records), from which he was trying to learn English at the time of writing the play. It was not a great success on its first appearance in 1950, but was revived in 1957 in the 100-seat Théâtre de la Huchette in the then-edgy rue de la

Huchette (Arab cafés, jazz clubs and sleazy hotels: now wall-to-wall cheap eateries for tourists). It has never closed, and can still be seen there, in the same fifty-year-old production: Paris's equivalent of *The Mousetrap.* Ionesco's later plays are darker, introducing violence, fear and anguish at the impossibility of communication. Even grimmer are those of **Samuel Beckett** (1906–89), an Irishman who wrote novels and plays in both French and English. But even at their darkest they are floated on cryptic eloquence and a haunting humour, which made his *Waiting for Godot* (1949), a chamber piece for four tramps and one tree, an unexpected success when it was revived in London with star actors in 2010. The last of the recognized 'theatre of the absurd' authors, **Arthur Adamov** (1908–70), was also foreign, born in Russia of Russian–Armenian parents. This is perhaps indicative of the long-standing attraction of Paris to foreign artists and writers, and also of French readers' and theatre-goers' growing receptivity to their work. Indeed there have been few notable French-born playwrights working in the post-war period at all. One was Genet. His deliberately unnerving plays are unrealistic in style and feature people shunned by bourgeois society (exploited maids who eventually murder their mistress in *Les Bonnes,* 1947; inmates and patrons of a brothel in *Le Balcon*, 1957; blacks in *Les Nègres*, 1959). Nevertheless they were successfully staged in the commercial theatre and filmed, and have often been revived in France and abroad.

The period from the end of the Second World War to the oil shock of 1973 is sometimes referred to in France as the 'Trente Glorieuses', the thirty glorious years. The glory in question was not military or artistic but economic: this was a period of continuous economic growth, during which the standard of living of French people rose in a way it had never done before. This new prosperity was overshadowed in the 1950s by the Algerian War. But De Gaulle's return to power in 1958, followed by the proclamation of a new republic, the Fifth, and the end of the draining war in 1962, introduced a period of fifty years of political stability and considerable prosperity continuing to the present day: something that France had not enjoyed since 1789. Yet this material progress has been accompanied by a loss of cultural influence on the rest of the world. Artists no longer feel the compulsion to come to Paris to paint, or writers to write, as they did in the 1920s, or even in the 1950s, and intellectual fashions are now more likely to originate in London, New York or further afield than in the Quartier Latin or Saint-Germain.

Novel and film

The last internationally influential French novelists were the practitioners of what is still called the 'nouveau roman', though it is now what French people call 'neuf à la façon du Pont Neuf', new like the New Bridge (the oldest bridge in Paris). The heyday of this school was the 1950s and 1960s, when most of these novelists were published by the Editions de Minuit, a house that was also gaining notoriety at the time by publishing pamphlets against the Algerian War. The group was given its name, as so often happens, by a hostile reviewer in 1957, but the challenge was picked up by **Alain Robbe-Grillet** (1922–2008) in 1963 when he published a collection of essays, many of which had appeared earlier in literary journals, under the manifesto title *Pour un nouveau roman*. The 'new' novel was to be new by discarding what had been considered the key elements of the 'old' novel: plot, 'believable' characters, psychological analysis. Instead much attention was paid to the actual business of writing: the workings were to be shown on the surface, rather like the heating and ventilation pipes of the Centre Pompidou, that trophy building designed in 1970 and opened in 1977. Jean Ricardou, novelist and theorist, famously wrote that the novel would no longer be 'l'écriture d'une aventure', the writing(-up) of an adventure, but 'l'aventure d'une écriture'. Unsurprisingly, the mass readership was less than ready to follow the novelists on this adventure. The chief novelists whose names are associated with the 'nouveau roman', as well as Robbe-Grillet, are **Michel Butor** (1926–), **Marguerite Duras** (1914–96), **Claude Simon** (1913–2005) and the much older **Nathalie Sarraute** (1900–99), an émigrée from Russia naturalized and married in France, who published her first novels before the Second World War and remained faithful to the Gallimard stable. Many of these writers also worked in the cinema, writing scripts for Nouvelle Vague directors or even, like Robbe-Grillet and Duras, directing their own films.

Indeed, it was at this time that film became the 'cutting-edge' art form in France, endlessly discussed in newspapers, magazines and on the newly popular TV, and imitated abroad as far as Hollywood itself. Like the 'nouveaux romanciers', the directors of the Nouvelle Vague wanted to break with the old style of filmmaking, the 'cinéma de papa' as they called it, with its careful plotting, easily comprehensible characters, familiar stars, elaborate studio sets and highly professional camerawork. In came location shooting, hand-held camerawork (helped by the much lighter cameras that were now being produced), vague or barely existent plotting and little-known actors who soon became even more famous than the stars of the previous generation. All of these things are perfectly illustrated by Jean-Luc Godard's *A Bout de souffle* (Breathless, 1960) or François Truffaut's *Les Quatre cents coups* (The Four Hundred Blows, 1959), which still seem as fresh as if they were made yesterday. (Both titles were very badly translated: 'à bout de souffle' means 'completely out of breath, on the verge of collapse', something like 'beat' in the original American sense, while 'faire les quatre cents coups' means to keep behaving badly and getting into trouble, as the juvenile hero of the film does.) Most Nouvelle Vague films have not worn so well as these: many, so exciting at the time, can now seem scrappy and irritating, while the best of the 'cinéma de papa' has in the end lasted better (though to be fair, it is only the cream of these productions that is shown any longer).

'French Theory'

France's last cultural export of significance was what is given the generic name of 'French Theory'. The writers bundled together under this title, I believe, fall outside the scope of this book, belonging more to history, philosophy and psychology. Of the most famous names, **Roland Barthes** (1915–80), **Michel Foucault** (1926–84), **Jacques Derrida** (1930–2004) and the much older **Jacques Lacan** (1901–81, the subject of another book in this series), it is Barthes' ideas that have the most direct bearing on the study of literature, and so will be touched upon briefly here. Each of the four writers mentioned had a different background and, originally, different academic interests: Barthes in literature (originally classics), Foucault history, but soon moving to philosophy and psychology, Derrida philosophy, and Lacan psychology and psychoanalysis. They came to know each other in middle life (Barthes and Foucault served together on the founding committee of the journal *Critique*, for example), but were never a close-knit 'school' like, say, the Naturalists. The important thing to bear in mind about their theoretical approach is that it is purely theoretical: at no point does it have to be tested, or indeed to interact with reality at all. Earlier theoreticians (with the possible exception of Rousseau) had typically produced theories that were founded on experience in a given field – Corneille's dramatic theory, for example, or Zola's theory of the novel – and that were intended to help the reader produce a better play or a better novel in the future. 'French Theory' is not of this kind. What it offers is new ways of *talking* about things. Theories can be borrowed from any field of endeavour and applied in any other: in the 1960s the vogue was for borrowing approaches from linguistics (structuralism, semiotics) and applying them to literature, history or social science, but in more recent times even quantum theory has been pressed into service. When one has mastered the technical vocabulary of these writers (different for each one), what can one do with it? What but write essays, then a thesis, then perhaps lectures? The home of 'French Theory' is the university, and, so far, definitely the Anglo-Saxon rather than the French university.

The most approachable of the 1960s theorists is certainly Roland Barthes. His name is associated with two formulae of that time: the 'death of the author' and 'readerly versus writerly texts'. 'La mort de l'auteur' was the title of an essay he published in 1968. It is not, of course, about the death of any real author, or of authors as a class: instead it takes issue with the idea, then still predominant in French school and university teaching, that the most important thing about any text was its author, what we could learn about him (nearly always him), his life and his intentions in writing the work in question. This idea had been criticized long before: by Proust, for example, in *Contre sainte-Beuve* (written in 1908–9 but not published until 1954), or Paul Valéry in *Tel quel*, a collection of earlier essays published in 1925. Among English-speaking critics, Wimsatt and Beardsley had demolished the idea that literary reading was a matter of searching out the author's intention, in their famous chapter 'The Intentional Fallacy' in *The Verbal Icon* (1954).

We even remember the young Rimbaud protesting, 'J'ai voulu dire ce que ça dit', in the 1870s. But Barthes gave these ideas new, forceful expression – he was a witty, trenchant writer and lecturer, particularly in his early days – and the time was obviously right for their reception. 1968 was, after all, the year when French students briefly revolted and demanded, among other things, a change to the old, authoritarian style of teaching at the Sorbonne and elsewhere. Barthes's reading method offered more autonomy and power to the reader, inviting him to construct his own reading of the text. This must imply reduced authority for the author: as Barthes wrote, 'la naissance du lecteur doit se payer de la mort de l'auteur' (the birth of the [active, engaged] reader has as its price the death of the author).

He returns to this idea in a short work of 1973, *Le Plaisir du texte*, where he draws a distinction between a text that is *lisible* (literally, readable) and one that is *scriptible* (an invented word that, if it existed, would mean 'writeable'). These words have been rather badly translated into English as 'readerly' and 'writerly'. A 'lisible' text is one that can be read easily, without really being aware that one is reading, a book to lose oneself in: nearly all fiction before 1950 was, Barthes thinks, of this kind. A 'scriptible' book demands more work: it will probably keep reminding us that this is a book and that we are reading. As readers, we have to, as it were, also be writing the book as we go along. (There is a striking similarity here to the distinction Brecht made between bourgeois drama, aimed at consumers, and the kind of play he wished to write, which demanded active spectators.) Barthes asserts that while the first kind of book gives us 'plaisir', pleasure, only the second kind gives 'jouissance' – fully satisfying, orgasmic pleasure (the usual translation, 'bliss', is quite misleading). It is doubtful how many readers would agree, but most 'literary' novels written in the 1960s and 1970s tried to be, in at least some measure, 'scriptibles'. Barthes was also a pioneer of the extension of semiotics, the study of signs, from its home in linguistics to much wider fields. He studied the varied messages of dress (here again forestalled by Balzac in his *Traité de la vie élégante* of 1830), took an amused interest in the language of advertising and enjoyed uncovering hidden meanings in fields as varied as food ('Le bifteck'), wrestling or striptease. The short essays, only two or three pages each, in which he discusses these things were collected in *Mythologies* (1957), and form a good introduction to his outlook and early style.

Later novelists

Notable novelists of the 1970s include **Michel Tournier** (1924–) and **Georges Perec** (1936–82). Tournier writes in a traditional style (i.e. 'lisible' rather than 'scriptible'), but of strange and sometimes horrifying events and characters. His first published novel, *Vendredi, ou les limbes du Pacifique* (Friday, or the lost world of the Pacific, 1967) is based on *Robinson Crusoe,* while his best, *Le Roi des aulnes* (1970), takes its title from Goethe's poem 'The Erl-King'. Set in the Second World War, its central figure is a carrier-off of children who is somehow both sinister and beneficent. Tournier also wrote short stories, and one of his collections, such as *Le Coq de bruyère* (The Grouse, 1978), could be a good introduction to his themes and style. Perec, on the other hand, is a deliberately experimental writer: his early novel *La Disparition* (The Disappearance, 1969), for example, was written in its entirety without using the letter 'e'. Later works like *W ou le souvenir d'enfance* (1975), or *La vie mode d'emploi* (Life, the instruction manual, 1978) have more human appeal, and won him greater recognition before his sadly early death from cancer.

Since roughly 1980, many of the conditions of production of literature have changed. The 'avant-garde' world, as it existed from the 1890s to the 1960s, seems to have little life left in it: the little magazines have been dying off and small publishers have been bought up by media conglomerates, often losing their risk-taking commissioning editors in the process. What survives in the mass media is the twentieth-century notion that every new work should be entirely original, and if possible shocking. But to really 'épater le bourgeois' (shock the bourgeois) has long been a hopeless aspiration: the bourgeois simply rolls over and begs 'shock me some more'. When Raymond Queneau spoke in the 1950s of the need to 'décaper la littérature de ses rouilles diverses, de ses croûtes' (strip literature of its various rusts and scabs), he was using a live metaphor: 'un décapant' (no adjective listed in the Robert dictionary of 1970) was 'un produit servant à décaper' – something like paint-stripper. Now every other notice of a play or comedy show uses the adjective 'décapant' (abrasive, caustic) as a term of praise, confident that it will attract audiences.

Writers of the late twentieth century and the present day show little interest in the technical devices so important in the 'nouveau roman'. 'Lisibilité' has to some extent returned to the 'literary' novel (from the commercial novel, of course, it had never gone away). Successful forms include the first-person story with some autobiographical content, now christened 'auto-fiction', and accounts of family life and disappearing social milieux. The most famous exponent of these genres is **Annie Ernaux** (1940–). Others include **Pierre Bergounioux** (1949–), **Catherine Millet** (1948–) and **Christine Angot** (1959–).

In recent times, academics in France, England and the USA have begun to take an increased interest in literature produced in the former French colonies, both before and after independence. Many important works were produced long before independence by such writers as the poets **Léopold Sédar Senghor** (1906–80), who became the first President of Senegal, and **Aimé Césaire** (1913–2008) of Martinique, who in fact studied together at the Ecole Normale Supérieure in Paris. The novel *Rue Cases-Nègres* (1950) by the Martiniquais novelist **Joseph Zobel** (1915–2004), made into a delightful film in 1983, gives a vivid picture of harsh life on the sugar plantations, but also of the educational opportunities the French system offered to a tiny intellectual elite.

African writers read and admired in France from the 1950s onwards include the Senegalese **Ousmane Sembène** (1923–2007), also a filmmaker, **Mariama Bâ** (1929–81) and the Guinean **Laye Camara** (1928–80), author of the very popular 'auto-fiction' *L'Enfant noir* (1953), then simply called a novel. Still publishing is the Algerian novelist **Assia Djébar** (1936–), elected to the Académie Française in 2005, while one of the most successful writers of the 1980s was **Tahar ben Jelloun** (1944–), a Moroccan-born novelist and essayist who writes chiefly in French but also in Arabic. Like many of France's post-colonial writers, he was a product of the international *Lycée Français* system. Apparently he is now the French writer most translated into other languages.

Most critics would not class Camus or Marguerite Duras as 'colonial' writers, though both grew up in the colonies and set many of their best-known writings there (Camus' *L'Etranger* is set in Algiers and *La Peste* in Oran, Duras's *Un barrage contre le Pacifique* and *L'Amant* in Indo-China).

Novelists born in the late 1950s or 1960s and active today include, among the best known, **Michel Houellebecq** (1956–), who first achieved notoriety for his sexual explicitness of a non-PC kind with *Les particules élémentaires* (1998) and continued in the same vein with *Plateforme* (2001) and *La possibilité d'une île* (2005). He seems finally to have achieved respectability in 2010, winning the Prix Goncourt (France's most prestigious literary prize) with *La carte et le territoire*. **Frédéric Beigbeder** (1965–) published his first three novels in the 1990s, but achieved fame with *Windows on the World* (2003) set in the restaurant of that name in the World Trade Center on the morning of 11 September 2001. His most recent and extremely successful novel is the 'auto-fiction' *Un roman français* (2009). Reflecting the much greater educational and publishing opportunities available to women in the later twentieth century, many of the most successful writers of this period are female, and are styled by the politically correct 'auteures' or 'écrivaines' (just when their English-speaking sisters are refusing to be known as 'actresses' or, heaven forbid, 'authoresses'). Recognized women writers of this age-group include **Christine Angot** (1959–), the Belgian **Amélie Nothomb** (1967–), regarded by some as not entirely serious because of her great productivity (one or more novels every year), **Marie N'Diaye** (1967–), despite her African name entirely French by upbringing and literary choices, or **Marie Darrieussecq** (1969–), a psychoanalyst and novelist almost as productive as Nothomb.

Twentieth-century literary writing, determinedly transgressive in the first sixty or so years of the century, is not so easy to characterize in the latter part, no doubt in part because shock value is no longer so easy to cultivate. But there is still a self-defining 'literary' world, consciously setting itself apart from mass tastes. What may become of that world in the new century is what we shall now very briefly look at.

Conclusion: the twenty-first century: literature after paper?

French literary culture at its pinnacle is still in some respects very traditional. The Académie Française, founded in 1635, still meets in the magnificent buildings of 1680 assigned to it in 1795, its forty members ('les Immortels', elected for life) wearing on ceremonial occasions the heavily embroidered green uniforms ('l'habit vert') designed for them in the late eighteenth century, complete with sword. They are engaged on producing the ninth edition of their dictionary, supposedly the most authoritative account of correct usage. The first part (of the ninth edition) appeared in 1992, reaching *enzyme*, and in the ensuing eighteen years they have worked their way from *éocène* to *promesse*. The Comédie-Française is still performing the 'grands classiques' of the seventeenth century, though nowadays also foreign works in translation. Perhaps even more strikingly, the Lycée Louis-le-Grand, formerly the Collège de Clermont, where Molière, Voltaire, Diderot, Robespierre, Baudelaire, Hugo, Césaire, Sartre and Barthes all studied, is still functioning in mostly nineteenth-century buildings on its original site on the *cardo* (the north-south axis) of Roman Lutetia. It is one of the two most sought-after secondary schools in the country (the other, the Lycée Henri-IV, is about five minutes' walk away), taking an utterly disproportionate number of places in the competitive entrance examination for the Ecole Normale Supérieure (nursery of most of the twentieth-century philosophers), which with the other *grandes écoles* (professional schools) forms the main way into a steady and well-paid intellectual career.

These are all institutions that a nineteenth-century Frenchman would recognize, though he would be astonished to see women attending them. But the country they serve, and in particular the potential audience for literature, has changed and is changing in dramatic ways. First of all, written texts, and particularly written fiction, now have to compete with various visual media offering quicker stimulation, starting with the cinema (now more than a hundred years old), but now including television, DVDs, downloads and interactive video games. The French intellectual world has been quick to co-opt these as new 'arts': not only new films but also new computer games are given serious reviews in newspapers and magazines. Indeed film ('le 7e art') is now seen as an art under threat from newer media, and is subsidised and heavily promoted to children by schools as well as the cinema industry. But the most popular new films are usually American, dubbed or sub-titled. Both children and adults are keen consumers of stories in strip-cartoon form called BD *(bande dessinée),* sometimes referred to as 'le 9e art' (TV was the eighth). Even *A la recherche du temps perdu* has recently appeared in strip form. If one enters Gibert Joseph, the five-storey bookshop opposite the old Sorbonne site where generations of students have bought their texts, one finds that the whole of the ground floor is given over to BD albums. And on the 'literature' floor, the second, another surprise awaits. More shelves are given over to translations from other languages than to works originally written in French. Many French readers now seem happier reading translated than French work: not only children, who of course devour Harry Potter and the Twilight series along with their contemporaries around the world, but adults too.

Schools still try to support the reading of French literature: all school examinations, even the vocational ones, include a compulsory test of formal French, and usually the study of at least a handful of literary selections. But they face an uphill battle with a texting and tweeting generation of students. Also, fifty years of immigration have ensured that, in the cities and inner suburbs, the home language of many of their students is not standard metropolitan French, in which almost all published texts are still written. Gifted and committed teachers can face all these challenges and achieve the seemingly impossible: a recent film, *L'Esquive* (2004, translated in the US as 'Games of Love and Chance') shows a class of fifteen-year-old students, mostly of immigrant background, putting on a play by Marivaux, of all unlikely choices. But the difficulties remain, and are well illustrated by Laurent Cantet's 2008 film *Entre les murs* (The Class – literally 'Within the Walls').

New 'literary' novels usually sell poorly, unless they are nominated for or win one of the numerous prizes awarded every year, when their sales can increase ten or a hundredfold. It is still a ritual part of the *rentrée*, the slow return from the long summer holidays, to read the book or books of the year, and a very large proportion of new titles are published in time for September reviews, in the hope of catching these seasonal readers. Newly published poetry barely sells at all, but then it never has since the days of Victor Hugo and François Coppée. Performance poetry, called 'slam', is popular at present: it is staged in cafes and clubs, anyone can participate and there is drink and sometimes music.

In general, and particularly in Paris where the left-wing city council controls subsidies and venues, there seems to be a wish to deprofessionalize writing, to play down traditional French literary forms and promote new media and productions associated with the former colonies and the now large population of immigrant descent. The Paris equivalent of 'Poems on the Tube' are almost invariably very short, and usually by little-known or unknown writers.

Symbolic of changing tastes is the fate of the Gaîté Lyrique theatre, once run by Offenbach and the home of operetta in the twentieth century, which has just been converted by the city, in a programme taking years and costing millions, to be the home of 'les arts numériques': digital arts. Its programmes will include rock concerts and 'projections numériques': there is also a permanent bank of seventy screens on which visitors can play 'artistic' – i.e. not commercial – computer games.

In the face of all this, the fact that written texts may soon migrate from paper to electronic reading devices seems a relatively manageable change. But will people still want to read, to define themselves as readers and writers? The large number of people still to be seen reading books on the Metro (and they almost always are books so far, rather than other hand-held devices) suggests hope. But a certain relationship of the French to their literature does seem to be changing. The nineteen-year-old Rimbaud, still with only three or four poems published, when he had to fill in an official form described himself as an 'homme de lettres'. Will any twenty-first-century young men or women think of themselves in this way? The future will tell.

Making a start: suggestions for further reading

I have written this book on the assumption that anyone who bought it must at least have been considering reading some French literature. I hope that exposure to a few samples will have confirmed him or her in this plan. But where to begin?

A short book would obviously be a better start than a long one, and books written in the 'classical' period (seventeenth and eighteenth centuries) are usually easier than nineteenth- or twentieth-century ones, simply because they are shorter and have a more restricted vocabulary. Exceptions to this rule of thumb would be Stendhal in the nineteenth century (whose novels are long but much less linguistically difficult than those of Balzac or Flaubert), and Camus in the twentieth.

There is, of course, always the option of reading French works in English translation. As a translator myself, I can hardly complain if people do this. But I would urge anyone with a reasonable command of French to attempt the originals, perhaps with a translation at hand to refer to if things get too difficult. All of the books mentioned here, except some of the most recent, are available in translation, usually in Penguin Classics or Oxford World's Classics. Parallel text versions are very useful, but sadly few of these are published nowadays.

Texts

If one is embarking on French literature in French, the options are almost literally limitless. The national library, the Bibliothèque de France, plans to put most of its holdings in French – a million titles achieved so far – on the Gallica website, and it is beginning to make the more frequently read among them available as e-books. The most respected collection of classics, including modern classics, in print on paper is the Bibliothèque de la Pléiade, published by Gallimard, but these handsome, scholarly (and wonderfully portable) volumes are too expensive for most students. Almost all the works mentioned in this book will be found in one or more of the French paperback series. Garnier-Flammarion, Le Livre de Poche and Presses Pocket all offer introductions and notes (Garnier-Flammarion to my mind usually the best: Presses Pocket notes are aimed at upper secondary students). A most valuable offshoot of Le Livre de Poche is their Lettres Gothiques series, offering medieval works with modern French versions in parallel text. Rabelais's *Pantagruel* and *Gargantua* are available in this series. Finally, really cheap texts without notes (a couple of euros apiece) can be had in the Librio series: these are usually popular single texts by classic writers such as Molière's *Tartuffe* or Voltaire's *Candide,* but some are interesting short collections of material that would otherwise be very hard to find (e.g. soldiers' letters home from the First World War).

Background and guides

Readers seeking further information about the books and authors discussed here will no doubt start with the internet. I have found Wikipedia entries to be mostly accurate as to content. But for interpretative and critical approaches, they will still have to head to the library. An excellent book on the dictionary plan which does not, however, restrict itself to material facts is the *New Oxford Companion to Literature in French* edited by Peter France – no longer so new, since it appeared in 1995, but still well worth consulting.

Translations in the Penguin Classics or Oxford World's Classics series will have informative and sometimes thought-provoking introductions, and suggestions for further reading.

The 'Critical Guides to French Literature' series published by Grant & Cutler in the 1980s and 1990s (the last few in the early 2000s) are introductions, mostly reliable, to individual texts: there is, I think, a volume on every work considered at any length in this book.

I should like to mention here one general work that I greatly admire, and have recommended to students over my years of teaching. It is *Mimesis*, by Erich Auerbach, first published in German in 1946, but in fact written in wartime conditions (and hence to a large extent from memory) in Istanbul in 1942–3. Translated into English and published by the Princeton University Press in 1953, it has never been out of print since. It contains excellent chapters on the Chanson de Roland (5), on a *roman* by Chrétien de Troyes (6), on Rabelais (11) and Montaigne (12). Later chapters are even more far-reaching. Chapter 15, 'The *Faux Dévot*', begins with La Bruyère but expands to take in Molière, Racine and seventeenth-century French literature in general, while chapter 16, 'The Interrupted Supper', moves from *Manon Lescaut* to Voltaire and Saint-Simon. Chapter 18, 'In the Hôtel de La Mole', begins with Julien and Mathilde from *Le Rouge et le Noir* but is soon discussing Stendhal, Rousseau, Romanticism, Balzac and Flaubert. Chapter 19 begins with the Goncourts' *Germinie Lacerteux,* but also treats Zola at length before ending with the German realists and the Russians Turgeniev, Tolstoy and Dostoevsky. Other chapters discuss Italian, Spanish and

English authors. *Mimesis* is indeed a *tour de force*. Clearly the work of a strikingly perceptive reader who was also an extraordinarily well-read man, its 550 pages do not boast a single footnote.

The following notes do not include full histories of literature, or of particular centuries, or academic studies of authors. Students will find these in their reading lists. I simply refer to works that I have found interesting and useful, and which may appeal to readers not making a formal study of French literature.

Sixteenth century

A good background to sixteenth-century texts is Elizabeth L. Eisenstein, *The Printing Revolution in Early Modern Europe* (1983, paperback edition 2005 still in print). Her chapter 4, 'The Expanding Republic of Letters', traces its theme as far forward as the eighteenth century.

The Penguin Classics translations by M.A. Screech of Rabelais and Montaigne (both the *Essays* and the *Apologie de Raymond Sebond* as a single volume) have very full and admirably learned introductions, written from the point of view of the translator as a committed Christian.

There has been a remarkable revival of interest in Montaigne in very recent years, with several young or youngish authors trying to engage with the essayist in the way he would have wished, as a fellow human being rather an embalmed 'classic'. Sarah Bakewell's admirable *How to Live: a life of Montaigne in one question and twenty attempts at an answer* (2010) has been a publishing success, winning several prizes. The communication project Oxford Muse, founded by the distinguished historian of France Theodore Zeldin, is now inviting readers at large to emulate Montaigne and contribute brief self-portraits to a common database.

Seventeenth century

Peter Burke, *The Fabrication of Louis XIV* (1994), is a valuable study of the different ways in which the king's image was deliberately constructed over the course of his reign. Georgia Cowart, *The Triumph of Pleasure: Louis XIV and the Politics of Spectacle* (2008), focusses chiefly on opera and ballet.

Paul Bénichou's classic study of the 'classical' writers in their social and ethical context, *Morales du grand siècle* (1948), was translated by Elizabeth Hughes as *Man and Ethics: Studies in French Classicism* (1971).

Eighteenth century

Robert Darnton's works of French cultural history offer an interesting background to the literature of the century (*The Great Cat Massacre and Other Episodes in French Cultural History,* 1984; *The Business of Enlightenment: A Publishing History of the Encyclopédie,* 1987).

Well-researched as well as engagingly written are Nancy Mitford's biographies of Madame de Pompadour (1954) and Voltaire (1957).

Bertrand Russell declared that he had intended his *History of Western Philosophy* (1946) as a work of social history rather than a technical contribution to philosophy. It is clearly and attractively written but just as clearly biased against the philosophers he disapproved of. It contains a memorable hatchet-job on Rousseau.

Nineteenth century

For the nineteenth century, Graham Robb in his biographies of Balzac (1994), Hugo (1997) and Rimbaud (2000) not only writes

authoritatively about these authors, but gives an excellent introduction to the literary world of their day. A short and not obviously academic book, though it was composed by an Oxford
don, is Robert Baldick, *Dinner at Magny's* (1971, Penguin 1973,
now out of print but available in libraries or from online booksellers). In it Baldick attempts to reconstitute the conversation
between the writers (Flaubert, the Goncourts, Sainte-Beuve,
Gautier, Turgenev and, on one occasion only, George Sand) who
used to meet for private dinners at Magny's restaurant in Paris in
the 1860s. Every speech ascribed to them has its origins in the
Goncourts' journals, Flaubert's letters or some other such contemporary source, yet the book reads remarkably convincingly as
a series of real conversations, and gives an eye-opening introduction to the attitudes, political, sexual and to writing, of successful
authors at that time. It may perhaps offer a partial answer to
why there were so few successful women writers in the French
nineteenth century.

In the 1960s Paul Bénichou, born in 1908 and previously
known as a scholar of French classical literature, began a huge
research project on Romanticism, which led to the publication
of five highly regarded books, from *Le sacre de l'écrivain* (1973) to
Selon Mallarmé (According to Mallarmé, 1995). Only the first has
so far been translated into English, by Mark K. Jensen as *The
Consecration of the Writer* (1999).

Twentieth century

An invaluable work on French writing and literary life in the
twentieth century, alas not yet available in English, is Michel
Winock, *Le siècle des intellectuels* (1997). It is in three sections, the
second called *Les années Gide* (the Gide years) and the third *Les
années Sartre*, but it also covers the emergence of 'theory' in the
1960s and 1970s and the complicated political involvements of

its exponents. Winock's twenty-page epilogue is entitled *La fin des intellectuels?*. Priscilla P. Clark, *Literary France: the Making of a Culture* (1987) is much shorter and more accessible: a good introduction to how 'literature' as an institution developed in France. There are brief and clear treatments of the more important French exponents of literary theory in Clare Connors, *Literary Theory: a Beginner's Guide* (2010).

Dominique Viart and Bruno Vercier, *La littérature française au présent* (2005, not yet translated) brings the story up to and past the millennium.

Produced to accompany a recent exhibition celebrating the centenary of the famous publishing house, Alain Jaubert and Brigitte Besse, *Portraits pour un siècle: cent écrivains* (Gallimard/BnF, 2011) commemorates a hundred authors (eighty-eight men and twelve women, seventy French and thirty foreign) published, and in many cases discovered, by Gallimard, and gives an idea of the controlling position the house held in the French literary world throughout the twentieth century. Each author is represented by a full-page photograph and a short text, and almost every author mentioned in our chapter 7 is included (all between pages 166 and 197, and many afterwards).

Authors on authors

Many of the authors discussed here have inspired other creative writers in French and also in other languages. As mentioned above, Sartre wrote psycho-biographies, on existentialist principles, of Baudelaire (1946) and Flaubert (*L'Idiot de la famille*, 1971–2). Both are available in English. *Baudelaire* is short and surprisingly accessible, *The Family Idiot* long (three volumes) and difficult.

To mention just a few writers in other languages, Angela Carter's short story 'Black Venus', in the 1985 collection of that name, rewrites the Baudelaire–Jeanne Duval relationship from the woman's point of view. Julian Barnes's novel *Flaubert's Parrot* (1984) is supposedly told by a Flaubert scholar planning a book on him: the parrot is the one that appears, transfigured, to Félicité at the end of *Un cœur simple*, or rather, one of the three stuffed parrots in various Rouen museums each purporting to be the original. Flaubert's *Madame Bovary* inspired the Peruvian novelist Mario Vargas Llosa to write *La orgia perpetua* in 1975 (translated by Helen Lane as *The Perpetual Orgy* in 1986). Despite its sensational title this is a literary essay, first discussing the special meaning the novel had for Vargas Llosa, and then embarking on a close technical account (Julian Barnes thought it the best in existence) of how it was written.

Biographies romancées of French authors by foreign novelists include a life of Molière by Mikhail Bulgakov, written in 1933 but published in Russian only in 1962, then translated into French and into English (1986). Bulgakov also wrote a play about Molière's struggles with the censors, which was banned after four performances, the Russian censors seeing too many parallels in it with the playwright's own situation.

The American novelist Edmund White has written thoughtful, personally involved biographies of Genet (1993), Proust (1998) and Rimbaud (2008).

I repeat, however: the best way to start is to get to grips with an original book, of whatever period or genre, and take things from there. Alan Bennett's short novel *The Uncommon Reader* (2007) offers an inspiring example of this method.

Index

Note: Page numbers for illustrations are shown in italics.